GLOBAL ALLIES

COMPARING US ALLIANCES
IN THE 21ST CENTURY

GLOBAL ALLIES

COMPARING US ALLIANCES
IN THE 21ST CENTURY

EDITED BY MICHAEL WESLEY

Australian
National
University

PRESS

ANU PRESS

Published by ANU Press
The Australian National University
Acton ACT 2601, Australia
Email: anupress@anu.edu.au
This title is also available online at press.anu.edu.au

National Library of Australia Cataloguing-in-Publication entry

Title: Global allies : comparing US alliances in the 21st century
            / Michael Wesley (editor).

ISBN: 9781760461171 (paperback) 9781760461188 (ebook)

Subjects: Balance of power.
            Alliances.
            United States--Foreign relations--Asia.
            United States--Foreign relations--Europe.
            United States--Politics and government--21st century.

Other Creators/Contributors:
            Wesley, Michael, 1968- editor.

Cover design and layout by ANU Press

Contents

List of Acronyms

A2AD	anti-area access and denial
AIIB	Asian Infrastructure Investment Bank
ANZUS	Australia, New Zealand, United States Security
ARF	ASEAN Regional Forum
ASEAN	Association of Southeast Asian Nations
BEAC	Barents Euro-Arctic Council
CFI	Connected Forces Initiative
CSIS	Center for Strategic and International Studies
DPJ	Democratic Party of Japan
DPRK	Democratic People's Republic of Korea (North Korea)
EAC	East Asian Community
FTA	free trade agreement
HADR	humanitarian assistance and disaster relief
ISAF	International Security Assistance Force
ISIS	Islamic State of Iraq and Syria
JEF	Joint Expeditionary Force
JUSMAGTHAI	Joint US Military Advisory Group Thailand
KFOR	Kosovo Force
LDP	Liberal Democratic Party (Japan)
NATO	North Atlantic Treaty Organization
NORDEFCO	Nordic Defence Cooperation
NUPI	Norwegian Institute of International Affairs

OSCE	Organization for Security and Co-operation in Europe
PRC	People's Republic of China
RoK	Republic of Korea (South Korea)
TIP	Trafficking in Persons
UNPROFOR	United Nations Protection Force
VJTF	Very High Readiness Joint Task Force
WTO	World Trade Organization

1

Global Allies in a Changing World

Michael Wesley

In October 2001, in response to the 9/11 terrorist attacks on the United States, US forces invaded Afghanistan, the country from which the attacks had been planned and coordinated. Operation Enduring Freedom, the invasion and subsequent stabilisation and state-building project in Afghanistan, saw the United States supported by the largest-ever coalition of its allies: 10 from Europe and two from Asia.[1] Over the next 13 years, US allies from Asia and Europe planned, fought and worked side by side in unprecedented numbers and intensity, battling a rising Taliban insurgency and supporting the consolidation of the Afghan Government and security forces. In the process, the North Atlantic Treaty Organization (NATO) in Europe and the San Francisco System in Asia became global allies, collaborating not only in Afghanistan but also in the stabilisation of Iraq, the setting up of the Proliferation Security Initiative to prevent transnational nuclear proliferation, and enforcing anti-piracy patrols in the Gulf of Aden. Japan, South Korea, Thailand, the Philippines, Australia, New Zealand and Pakistan were designated 'major non-NATO allies' and began attending issue-specific discussions among NATO members in Brussels.

---

1   Canada, although not in Europe, was a contributing NATO member; New Zealand, although no longer a member of ANZUS, had been designated a non-NATO ally by the administration of Bill Clinton in 1997.

A decade after the invasion of Afghanistan, in a speech to a joint sitting of the Australian parliament, US President Barack Obama proclaimed that 'the United States is turning our attention to the vast potential of the Asia Pacific region … the United States will play a larger and long-term role in shaping this region and its future'.[2] By mid-2012, the administration's resolve had been written into strategic policy: the United States would 'rebalance' its attention away from the Middle East towards the Asia-Pacific region, where 60 per cent of its naval, space and cyber assets would be positioned.[3] The American rebalance caused more than a ripple of disquiet among US allies in Europe. Many responded to the understandable implication that a rebalance towards Asia would mean a diminution of America's commitment to its security partnerships elsewhere. For many NATO members, the Chinese challenge to America's Pacific primacy was remote, whereas Russia's increasingly assertive and aggressive policies towards its near neighbours, Georgia, the Ukraine and NATO members in the Baltic states, represented the most profound challenge to European security since the end of the Cold War. Ironically at the same time in Asia, many security elites expressed scepticism about the seriousness of the rebalance. They questioned whether the United States would really be able to disentangle its forces and attention from the ongoing instability in the Middle East and North Africa and, even if it could, whether it would have the resolve to face down an increasingly confident and demanding China in the western Pacific. These concerns are likely to continue given the US air campaign against the Islamic State of Iraq and Syria (ISIS), and its recent recommitment of forces to Europe in the aftermath of Russian aggression in Ukraine.

Thus, in the first decade of the 21st century, US allies in Europe and Asia had traced the full arc of their new condition of interdependence, first tasting the benefits of collaboration and solidarity; and then the anxieties of competing for US commitment, attention and resources. Never before had NATO and the San Francisco system been so mutually significant. In 1949, the United States reversed 150 years of eschewing alliances by agreeing to a multilateral pact to shore up postwar Europe against an antagonistic and expansive Soviet Union. At the time, Washington had categorically ruled out a similar commitment in Asia, and rebuffed

---

2   'Text of Obama's Speech to Parliament', *Sydney Morning Herald*, 17 Nov. 2011, www.smh.com.au/national/text-of-obamas-speech-to-parliament-20111117-1nkcw.html.
3   US Department of Defense, 'Sustaining US Global Leadership: Priorities for 21st Century Defense', p. 2.

attempts by anxious wartime partners, such as Australia, to be allowed inside the NATO tent, at least at a consultative level. Gradually, however, whether as a condition for a peace deal with a rehabilitated Japan, or under the threat of communist expansion into the Pacific, it reneged, signing a series of alliances with Japan, South Korea, Taiwan, the Philippines, Thailand, Australia and New Zealand from 1951. Unlike NATO, these would be bilateral (or trilateral, in the case of Australia, New Zealand, United States Security (ANZUS)), and their operative clauses in general much less compelling as security guarantees than NATO's Article 5.

For the next half-century, the two alliance systems operated in isolation. While some NATO members joined the United Nations' enforcement action in Korea in the 1950s, it was not a NATO operation. None of the San Francisco allies showed the slightest interest in supporting the Asian commitments of European powers, even though Britain contributed to the postcolonial stabilisation and defence of Malaya. The Vietnam War in the 1960s and 1970s mobilised the San Francisco allies minus Japan, but not a single NATO member. Iraq's invasion of Kuwait in 1990 saw US allies from Europe and Asia come together to support a UN enforcement operation, as in Korea, but the experience was brief and had little effect on the different worlds of the two alliance systems. NATO became consumed by its post–Cold War expansion and the wars of the former Yugoslavia, while the San Francisco system seemed in decline, with Taiwan's loss of its formal alliance with the United States in 1978, New Zealand's expulsion from ANZUS in 1986, and the closure of US bases in the Philippines in 1992. As the new century dawned, it was not an attack on any smaller ally, but on the superpower anchor of both alliance systems that brought about a new era of interdependence. Suddenly the rationale of both alliance systems had shifted from deterring and defeating state-based aggression to addressing state dysfunction and battling transnational violent extremism. The new reality in a unipolar world was that allies of the sole superpower had to anticipate, understand and integrate with their major ally's new strategic imperatives. As a wounded America rose in fury, its long-time allies faced a choice of rising with it or being cast aside. For the first time, the thoughts and actions of remote US allies on the other side of the world became of abiding importance.

The Global Allies Project, on which this volume is based, brought together strategic scholars from eight countries allied to the United States to discuss challenges in alliance dynamics and management. The project is a response to a major lacuna in this new era of alliance interdependence.

While today America's European and Asian allies are intimately aware of each other's thinking on terrorism and counterinsurgency, counter-proliferation, piracy and sea-lane security, cyber-threats and hybrid challenges, there has been remarkably little discussion of the challenges of alliance management among the allies of the United States. While there are large and inevitable differences between different alliances, there are also significant commonalities, including dilemmas of commitment, trust and risk management, the difficulties of managing American expectations and domestic political resistance, issues of defence spending and interoperability, and reconciling alliance commitments with other foreign policy interests. For 60 years, US allies have managed these issues in mutual isolation, and sometimes in competition with each other. The Global Allies Project seeks to add a crucial tile to the alliance interdependence puzzle, by systematically comparing the challenges and processes of alliance management across a range of long-standing US allies in Europe and Asia.

Rather than look backwards, however, the Global Allies Project looks toward the future of alliance management in Europe and Asia. While it is impossible to tell whether another 9/11 will happen to reinforce the interoperation of Asian and European allies of the United States, we believe there are structural forces at play that will reinforce the interdependence of the two alliance systems, and that make the case for comparing alliance management dynamics an enduring one. It is the purpose of this introductory chapter to explore what some of these structural forces are. In the sections ahead, I examine the imperatives of alliance policy in an era of relative US power decline, of regional and global order challenges by revanchist powers, and of the changing balance of costs and benefits in alliance commitments. Rather than establish a framework for the detailed alliance-specific case studies that follow, this chapter is intended to set the general scene against which those case studies can be read.

Declining Relatives

The perennial debates about the relative decline of American power serve to underline how central US primacy has been for the post–World War II global order. The unprecedented and probably never-to-be replicated post–World War II power lead that allowed the United States to craft a world order according to its preferences, convince a large number of other states of its legitimacy, and defend it against its opponents, has been eroding steadily over the past 70 years. The collapse of the Soviet Union led to two decades of unipolarity but, unlike after World War II, the United States was not able to craft a stable or enduring 'new world order' as its first post–Cold War president promised. Indeed, the past two decades have demonstrated the complexity and intractability of threats to world order and the limits of American power to craft durable solutions to them.

Perhaps the greatest challenge to American primacy has been the pervasive uncertainty within its own policymaking system about what US power can achieve and how and when it should be wielded. As the dust of the Soviet collapse settled, Washington was nonplussed at the seeming puniness of those challengers that arose in defiance of George HW Bush's new world order: a jumped-up Iraqi strongman; Serbian paramilitary thugs; an unhinged, jumpsuit-wearing North Korean dictator; and drug-addled Somali gangs. But, despite not even approaching the seriousness of the Cold War's crises, these new challenges would prove anything but routine matters for the sole superpower. American forces had little trouble in winning kinetic victories; what American power couldn't achieve was enduring solutions that were acceptable to liberal consciences or the liberal order. What these frustratingly enduring challenges produced was a rising tide of criticism within the US of how those in charge of US foreign policy were handling the sword and shield of the Republic.

And so, American foreign policy lurched between extremes of aggression and restraint as the 21st century began. The George W Bush administration brought to power a critical mass of neoconservatives who believed that it was imperative to use the unipolar moment to reshape the world for another era of American dominance and liberal peace. American power could not only recast an infinitely pliable world, it could create new realities. Those who resisted would be crushed, those who objected would be cast aside; those who were onboard would benefit from the new reality. But the early swagger of the neoconservatives turned sour as global opinion turned against the projected invasion of Iraq, and as coalition troops in both Afghanistan and Iraq faced rising insurgencies. The 2008 presidential election campaign saw both Republican and Democratic contenders criticise the Bush administration's recklessness in its use of force, its rhetorical excesses, and its cavalier treatment of long-time allies and partners of the United States. Bush's successor, Barack Obama, replaced confrontation with conciliation with those seen to be resisting the liberal global order—the Muslim world, China, Russia, Iran—and became as hesitant to use force as his predecessor had been bellicose.

Yet Obama's foreign policy registered few successes. Despite his search for a series of 'resets', Russia, China and Iran became more assertive and defiant and a series of Muslim states in the Middle East and Africa succumbed to an even more brutal jihadist insurgency. The candidates in the 2016 presidential election have united in distancing themselves from the Obama approach to the use—and particularly the non-use—of American power.

The backdrop to the oscillation of approaches to American power has been the slow vanishing of the unipolar era due to a combination of factors. One was the real demonstration of the limits of American power in Afghanistan and Iraq; unlike the Vietnam War, which was a proxy conflict against two Cold War opponents, these have been 21st-century insurgencies combining a millennial ideology, brittle structures of domestic order, deep sectarian divisions, and global support networks facilitated by new social media. The United States ran down its stocks of goodwill, public support, defence financing and tolerance for casualties, while the challenges of state dysfunction and Islamist insurgencies continue unabated. Meanwhile the global financial crisis mired the United States, Europe and Japan in debt, while dealing a major blow to the legitimacy of Western liberal dominance of the global economy. In the aftermath of the crisis, it became less and less controversial to observe the growing economic heft of emerging economies, particularly in Asia; on current trends, the United States will yield its century-long position as the world's largest economy during this decade. China is already the world's largest economy in purchasing power parity terms, the world's largest importer of minerals and energy, the world's largest exporter, the world's largest manufacturer, the world's largest trading nation, and the primary trading partner for 130 countries. In the meantime, its military spending has been increasing rapidly, leading some observers to argue that China represents a more profound threat to US primacy than the Soviet Union ever did.

At this time of relative decline, the United States faces some profound challenges to the liberal global order it founded. The Arab 'Spring' of 2009–11 did not bring about a spread of representative democracy in the Middle East but, rather, the collapse of political order amid a virulent fanatical insurgency, deepening sectarian divisions and the growing assertiveness of regional powers. The global financial crisis bequeathed a chronically weak and unstable global economy, in which the status quo powers in the international economic order are faced with mounting debt and pervasive weaknesses in their currencies, and more and more countries are looking to decidedly illiberal means of returning to stability and growth.[4] Meanwhile, three powers have begun new forms of military adventurism across the Eurasian landmass. Using the pretext of protecting ethnic Russian minorities outside its borders, Russia launched attacks on Georgia in 2008 and Ukraine in 2014, dismembering parts of both states' territories. In the aftermath of the invasions of Afghanistan and Iraq, Iran used the resulting chaos to extend its influence into Iraq, Syria, Lebanon and Yemen. Iranian forces are currently at war in Iraq, Syria and Yemen. In eastern Asia, China asserted territorial claims in the East China Sea and the South China Sea and across the line of control with India. Taken together, these actions represent a challenge to the territorial order across Asia, agreed in 1991 in Europe, 1915 in the Middle East and 1945 in East Asia. And each of these three revisionist powers, having closely watched US air and sea power in action since the end of the Cold War, has been patiently building up its anti-area access and denial (A2AD) capabilities—a development that has created an uncertainty of response in the United States and its allies. Finally, the world now faces new threats to the global information commons. The increasingly interconnected information and control systems of societies have proven extremely vulnerable to criminal and coercive attack; at the same time, the resort of major states to authoritarian control over their information systems threatens a possible Balkanisation of the global information network.

The combination of falling US relative power and rising systemic threats to that power creates a paradox of rising indispensability and falling credibility for the United States among its allies. On the one hand, Washington is unsure whether a decisive show of resolve will only further illustrate the ineffectiveness of US power *a la* Iraq and Afghanistan; on the other, each case of perceived American hesitance is taken as more evidence of the recession of American primacy. Meanwhile, American allies face challenges to the liberal order with a growing sense that any effective response must involve the full complement of allied commitment and solidarity, but such are the expectations of allies in Europe, Asia and the Middle East that the American response will almost inevitably be found wanting in each theatre. While Stephen Walt is right to observe that

---

4   The rise of statist economic models is the most prominent and worrying of these; see Ian Bremmer, *The End of the Free Market: Who Wins the War Between States and Corporations?*, New York: Portfolio, 2010.

hard balancing against the unipole is unlikely even under conditions of declining relative power, the dilemmas of alliance commitment and credibility are no less diminished.[5]

Shoring Up the Liberal Order

The frequency of US allies' and partners' recent exhortations on the need to defend the liberal order is a compelling sign that they are increasingly worried about its integrity. The states system seems to be under attack from above and below. In the Middle East and North Africa, jihadist insurgencies explicitly reject the borders drawn between Muslim societies. Their goal of a transnational caliphate, if successful, seeks to recast the postcolonial order across the Muslim world. In place of state territorial boundaries would be a single confessional divide between the society of believers and those of the unbelievers; across this divide would exist a state of perpetual war.

Empire states exist in the Caucasus and the Western Pacific that are determined to expand their boundaries, either through formal annexations of territory or through the creation of spheres of influence. President Vladimir Putin's Russia grieves the collapse of the Soviet Union and the loss of territory, in Europe and Central Asia, but especially in the Caucasus. Both Georgia and Ukraine made the fatal mistake of seeking to align their countries more with the West and less with Russia; such a challenge to the Russian sphere of influence was met by direct aggression and the annexation of strategically crucial territory. In the Western Pacific, China increasingly views the 'first island chain', stretching from Japan through the Ryukyus and Taiwan to the Philippines as a scheme imposed on it by the Western postwar settlement, to hem China in through an archipelago controlled by states hostile to it and allied with the United States. Beijing is increasingly intent on overturning this postwar settlement, absorbing Taiwan, building sea control in the South China Sea, and nibbling away at the Ryukyus via its claims to the Senkaku/Diaoyu Islands. As in the Caucasus, it is a process of challenging the status quo through unilateral and unpredictable *faits accompli*.

---

5   Stephen M Walt, 'Alliances in a Unipolar World', *World Politics*, vol. 61, no. 1, Jan. 2009, pp. 86–120. doi.org/10.1017/S0043887109000045.

In both Europe and Asia, the United States and its allies face a real paradox of liberal order maintenance that makes their commitments to uphold the liberal order both conditional and unconditional. The conditionality of the liberal order arises from its commitment to certain values, such as democracy, the rule of law and free assembly and exchange, as well as its belief that the liberal order will not be complete until there is universal adherence to these claims. Real problems arise when the liberal order is dependent on illiberal regimes for its stability. In these cases, support for authoritarian allies is always conditional and unpredictable; the fate of Egypt's President Hosni Mubarak showed that long-term US support can be suddenly withdrawn when one's authoritarian nature is suddenly on stark display. The parallel unconditionality of the liberal order arises from its commitment to liberal values and their eventual universality. This means that an attack on these values anywhere is taken to be an attack on them everywhere, creating mounting demands on the United States and its allies to 'do something' when these values are under assault. Whether or not actual strategic interests are at stake becomes secondary and, once committed to, the draining defence of liberal values becomes very hard to walk away from.

Both the conditionality and the unconditionality of liberal-order maintenance create real opportunities for those challenging the order. For a start, by definition these are states that do not identify with the order or its maintenance; they are able to free ride on those aspects they can benefit from, while avoiding, resisting or undermining elements they find threatening. The conditionality of US support for authoritarian or problematic allies creates opportunities for new partnerships, such as those developing between China and Saudi Arabia or between Russia and Pakistan. The unconditionality of US and allied commitments to defending liberal values generates a perpetual state of strategic chaos, as the upholders of the liberal order perpetually disperse their forces and resources based on maps not of interests but of values. The fanatical jihadists in the Muslim world can dependably draw the 'Great Satan' and its allies into what they believe to be a millennial battle on their own turf simply through a growing catalogue of outrages.

Alliance Costs and Benefits

The long history of regarding alliances in accounting terms, weighing up the costs and risks against the benefits and assurances they provide, is deeply embedded in political logics and the public mind. Arguably, one of the main reasons for the longevity of US alliances has been that their benefits have been seen to vastly outweigh their costs. For much of their history, US alliances have been relatively costless for both America and its allies. While it has become commonplace for American defence policymakers to complain of their allies' underspending on defence, there is little to suggest that America's alliance commitments contributed to higher US defence spending than would otherwise have been the case, while for much of their tenure, most US basing commitments in Asia and Europe have been financially supported by its smaller allies. For those smaller allies, there has rarely been any serious doubt that their alliances with the United States allowed them a level of security out of all proportion to their direct investments in the military and intelligence capabilities; or that an ending of their alliance with the United States would necessitate much greater defence expenditure to acquire the same level of protection.[6] Even when there were losses of blood and treasure in fighting alongside the United States in regional conflicts, smaller allies were aware that such exercises allowed their forces to maintain cutting-edge capabilities and their agencies access to inner realms of American intelligence and strategy.

An argument could be made that, for both America and its allies, there has been a convenient security–political trade-off to be made through their security relationships. Alliances in Asia and Europe provided the United States with political cover for its security commitments; the willingness of major powers to partner with US security commitments across the globe provided a sense of universal legitimacy to US strategic goals, both during the Cold War and after. For allies, the US guarantee provided security cover for their political alignments with the United States and the West; this meant that European states living under the shadow of the Iron Curtain and Asian states concerned about the spread of communist insurgencies could reassure themselves that they were safer as staunch members of the West than they would be if they tried to become neutral

---

6   Of course, there have been arguments that US alliances have actually detracted from allies' security by making them more prominent targets of attack.

and avoid the confrontation. Nor has there been a strong sense, on the part of the United States or its smaller allies, that the alliance has acted as a significant constraint on their freedom of foreign policy initiative.[7]

The politics of alliance maintenance have been subtle and varied across the various allied states. The virtues of American strategic power tend to erode quickly among both American and allied publics soon after that power is deployed. Consequently, alliance maintenance has always been an exercise in 'two-level games' in which allied governments must try to maintain domestic political acceptance for a range of alliance commitments that are regarded as acceptable by US policymakers.[8] Repeatedly, the two-level logic of alliance maintenance, in combination with the alliance accounting (or insurance) metaphor, has led to allies casting the alliance as the objective, rather than the means, of foreign and strategic policy. This meant that the United States was often joined in the exercise of coercion not because allies particularly subscribed to the objectives of coercion with the same intensity as the United States, but because they believed, and could argue to their publics, that 'alliance maintenance' required such a commitment to be shown.

There are three dangers in this approach. The first is that the alliance becomes heavily politicised. Controversial or costly actions taken in coalition with the intention of investing in alliance maintenance will end up increasing opposition to the alliance among both American and allied publics. The second cost is for the United States, because the imperative of alliance maintenance will mean that it finds itself paired with coalition partners who are less interested in the actual strategic objectives at hand than they are in keeping their major ally happy. This has been a problem in both Iraq and Afghanistan, where US allies have made decisions to pull out of operations long before the situation has been regarded as stable enough to justify withdrawal. The third danger of this approach to alliances is a tendency for both the United States and its allies to turn situations into tests of alliance credibility. The best example of this was the response to the 9/11 attacks, which the George W Bush administration clearly signalled was a test of how much allies were committed to American security and

---

7   See, for example, Michael Beckley, 'The Myth of Entangling Alliances: Reassessing the Security Risks of US Defense Pacts', *International Security*, vol. 39, no. 4, Spring 2015, pp. 7–48. doi. org/10.1162/ISEC_a_00197.
8   See Robert D Putnam, 'Diplomacy and Domestic Politics: The Logic of Two-Level Games', *International Organization*, vol. 42, no. 3, Summer 1988, pp. 427–60. doi.org/10.1017/S0020818300027697.

American global-order preferences. The result was broad buy-in to the invasion of Afghanistan, a country in which no Asian or European ally had any strategic stake. A couple of years later, Bush raised the alliance commitment bar by setting his sights on an invasion of Iraq, based on highly tenuous connections to the 9/11 attacks and global security more broadly. In this case, the Bush administration was in effect asking its allies not only to place their alliance ties above their own non-existent interests in Iraq, but also above their commitments to the rule of international law and the substantial opposition of their own populations. In the end, two European allies (Britain and Spain) and one Asian (Australian) joined the invasion, all three using the demonstration of their solidarity with Washington to gain significant concessions from a grateful Bush administration. Ultimately, perhaps reflecting some realism on the part of the Bush administration, there were few negative consequences for allies that did not join the Iraq invasion or its subsequent stabilisation phase.

There are signs that the relatively costless nature of alliances is starting to be questioned in both Europe and Asia. In the face of direct Russian and Chinese challenges to the status quo and to American primacy, both the United States and its respective allies are aware of difficult choices.[9] During the 2016 US presidential election campaign, Republican candidate Donald Trump committed to requiring US allies in Europe and Asia to pay more of the shared cost of their own security or risk the attenuation of those alliances. It remains to be seen whether the president will deliver on these pledges. Victor Cha observes that, in Asia, an alliance security dilemma has developed: whereas US-alliance-initiated regional efforts are portrayed as latent strategies for containing China, region-initiated attempts to engage China are seen as attempts to exclude the United States.[10] A similar situation may be emerging in Europe, where US initiatives aimed at deterring further Russian adventurism are being seen by some as only increasing Russian hostility, while European efforts to engage with Russia are seen by others to be weakening NATO. Beyond this, the utility of alliances is starting to be questioned. In Asia, every Chinese provocation is now taken as a litmus test of American resolve

---

9   See, for example, Stefanie V Hlatky & Jessica T Darden, 'Cash or Combat? America's Asian Alliances During the War in Afghanistan', *Asian Security*, vol. 11, no. 1, Mar. 2015, pp. 31–51. doi.org/10.1080/14799855.2015.1006360; Tongfi Kim, 'The Role of Leaders in Intra-Alliance Bargaining', *Asian Security*, vol. 10, no. 1, Mar. 2014, pp. 47–69. doi.org/10.1080/14799855.2013. 874338.
10   Victor D Cha, 'Complex Patchworks: US Alliances as Part of Asia's Regional Architecture', *Asia Policy*, no. 11, Jan. 2011, pp. 27–50.

and alliance commitment, a situation that bears heavily on American policymakers and cedes a great deal of initiative to Beijing. In Europe, there is a sense that NATO has been of little utility in dealing with three pressing challenges: the war in the Levant, Russian adventurism in the Caucasus, and the growing refugee crisis. It seems that alliances, so often seen as the ends of security policy, are now being found wanting as the means to greater security in more challenging security environments in both Europe and Asia.

Conclusion

Against this background, the comparison of alliance-management challenges faced by European and Asian allies of the United States unfolds as a rich exercise. While clearly acknowledging the differences between the two regions—the nature of treaty commitments, multilateralism versus bilateralism, strategic geography and levels of development—what has been truly fascinating has been the similarities between the two regions. Indeed, there have been more than a few points of convergence: the dilemmas of dealing with 'grey zone'/hybrid threats, the challenges of interoperability and the tension between regional and global focus for alliance action. But perhaps the most intriguing convergence has been in relation to alliance structures: whereas in Asia a system of bilateral alliances is slowly plurilateralising as US allies develop security partnerships with each other; in Europe there has been an observable process of NATO allies quietly developing their own bilateral security relationships with the United States.

The chapters that follow have been developed by security specialists and consider their own country's alliance with the United States. They constitute a rich collection of reflections on particular alliances, but arguably an even richer collective reflection on some of the generic challenges of managing well-matured alliances with the world's sole superpower.

2

Japan: From Passive Partner to Active Ally

HDP Envall

Japan is America's key ally in the Asia-Pacific, with the US–Japan alliance the foundation of America's role as a 'Pacific' power. Indeed, the United States 'has no better friend in the world than Japan'.[1] This important alliance emerged from Japan's defeat in World War II and the subsequent American-led occupation, but especially from America's shifting global strategy in the early Cold War. Increasingly tense relations with the Soviet Union, the communist victory in China and the Korean War pushed the United States to secure Japan within the Western bloc. The resulting strategic bargain between the two countries was for the United States to provide security for Japan, with Japan offering bases for the US military in return. The arrangement established Japan for the United States as a dependent security partner; however, it also allowed Japan to focus on the important postwar task of economic redevelopment.[2]

---

1   J Thomas Schieffer, 'Remarks Upon Arrival of the USS George Washington', Yokosuka, 25 Sep. 2008, viewed Aug. 2016, japan2.usembassy.gov/e/p/2008/tp-20080925-71.html.
2   Roger Buckley, *US–Japan Alliance Diplomacy, 1945–1990*, Cambridge University Press, 1992, pp. 28–29; Michael J Green, 'Balance of Power', in Steven K Vogel (ed.), *U.S.–Japan Relations in a Changing World*, Washington, DC: Brookings Institution Press, 2002, pp. 12–14; HDP Envall, 'Clashing Expectations: Strategic Thinking and Alliance Mismanagement in Japan', in Yoichiro Sato & Tan See Seng (eds), *United States Engagement in the Asia Pacific: Perspectives from Asia*, Amherst, NY: Cambria Press, 2015, pp. 66–67.

Despite facing some significant challenges, as well as considerable change in both countries, this structure has persisted largely intact over the subsequent 65 years. This continuity has, however, begun to give way over the past decade, especially in terms of how Japan envisages the alliance. During this period, and particularly since 2010, the emergence of a more contested order in the Asia-Pacific has prompted Japan to move away from its traditional acceptance of key asymmetries in the alliance. Japan is now seeking to distance itself from its role as a passive alliance partner and become a more active US ally.

This shift has been driven by the country's changing threat perceptions and the resulting recalculation of alliance risks. Japan—as with many junior allies—has always struggled to manage the dilemma between entrapment and abandonment, the 'secondary alliance' dilemma described by Glenn Snyder.[3] On the one hand, to rely excessively on the United States would be to risk becoming entrapped in American security engagements. On the other hand, however, to seek greater autonomy would be to risk being abandoned by the United States.[4] Over the past decade, Japan has come to perceive the risks of entrapment, even as they remain substantial and could potentially rise further, as less problematic than the risks presented by the changing balance of power (and threat) in the region and thus of abandonment.[5] In turn, this has pushed Japanese policymakers into revising the country's approach to international security and its role within the US alliance.

In order to explain Japan's experience of changing strategic conditions and security perceptions, this chapter assesses two interrelated dimensions of Japan's strategic calculations. It seeks primarily to understand how, in terms of domestic politics, Japan has approached its role in the alliance. But it also examines how Japan has managed its engagement of the wider regional context, especially in terms of the biggest change to the region— the rise of the People's Republic of China (hereafter China).[6] This chapter

---

3   See Glenn H Snyder, 'The Security Dilemma in Alliance Politics', *World Politics*, vol. 36, no. 4, 1984, pp. 466–68.

4   Green, 'Balance of Power', 2002, p. 14.

5   On increasing risks of abandonment and entrapment, see Nick Bisley, 'Securing the "Anchor of Regional Stability"? The Transformation of the US–Japan Alliance and East Asian Security', *Contemporary Southeast Asia*, vol. 30, no. 1, 2008, pp. 86–87. doi.org/10.1355/CS30-1D.

6   On the role of perceptions of power transition on dispute escalation between Japan and China, see Ryoko Nakano, 'The Sino–Japanese Territorial Dispute and Threat Perception in Power Transition', *Pacific Review*, vol. 29, no. 2, 2016, pp. 165–86. doi.org/10.1080/09512748.2015.1013 493.

examines the evolution of these two dimensions across three periods—the Cold War, the post–Cold War until 2010, and the newly contested order since 2010 characterised by the rise of a more assertive China.

The Cold War, 1951–89

Defeat in World War II, the experience of postwar occupation, and the new threats of the Cold War fundamentally reshaped Japan's security politics. The security role that Japan played in the emerging Cold War environment was influenced predominantly by the United States, its new ally. Accordingly, Japan adopted a pragmatic approach to its alliance with the United States and to its security policy more generally. As part of the grand bargain with the United States, Japanese Prime Minister Shigeru Yoshida established a security strategy that trod a line in domestic politics between what conservatives (rearmament) and progressives (unarmed neutrality) expected. Relying on the United States for security protection in return for bases meant that Yoshida could deliver something to both camps—security for the conservatives and a restriction on Japan's military capacity for the progressives. Yoshida's deft politics eventually developed into the orthodox consensus of Japan's Cold War security policy that came to be known as the Yoshida Doctrine.[7]

This doctrine provided Japan with a number of advantages throughout the Cold War. It allowed the country to focus on economic development after the devastation wrought by World War II rather than expend scarce resources on a quick military build-up. In what was a turbulent period of politics following the war, it also pushed the potentially divisive issue of defence to the periphery of Japanese politics. The capacity of alliance politics to destabilise Japanese politics would be briefly demonstrated by the US–Japan security treaty revision crisis of 1960. After this episode, however, Yoshida's successors in the ruling Liberal Democratic Party (LDP) were able to keep the politics of the US–Japan alliance largely out of Japanese politics. Most significantly for Japan's alliance policy, the Yoshida Doctrine made use of Article 9 of the Constitution, which prohibited Japan from maintaining a military for the purpose of making

---

7   Richard J Samuels, *Securing Japan: Tokyo's Grand Strategy and the Future of East Asia*, Ithaca, NY: Cornell University Press, 2007, pp. 29–37. On Yoshida's approach to postwar security politics, see also HDP Envall, 'Exceptions that Make the Rule? Koizumi Jun'ichirō and Political Leadership in Japan', *Japanese Studies*, vol. 28, no. 2, 2008, pp. 232–33. doi.org/10.1080/10371390802249198.

or threatening war. This was done as a way of resisting US pressure on Japan to contribute more as an ally. Entrapment in US security actions thus became less of a risk for Japan during the Cold War.[8]

Yet the Yoshida Doctrine also had its disadvantages. The first was that it institutionalised a Japanese dependence on the United States for the provision of security and overall strategic direction. This, in turn, meant a lack of autonomy for Japan in devising an international role for itself. The problem was recognised by Yoshida himself, who noted that the country would remain in a 'state of weakness' so long as it depended too heavily on the United States for its security.[9] It was also the target of key postwar prime ministers, such as Nobusuke Kishi and Yasuhiro Nakasone. They saw Japan's abrogation of its security role to the United States as a 'humiliation' and argued for Japan to adopt a more autonomous defence posture, even as they came around to supporting the US alliance at the core of Japan's national security policies.[10] Yoshida's approach also made Japan vulnerable to US accusations of 'free riding'; that is, benefiting from the security that America's engagement provided without contributing to the upkeep of this engagement. Criticism of this failing was especially pronounced from the 1970s. It forced Japan to respond by taking up a greater share of the cost of US bases in Japan and by redefining the idea of 'security' to include more of the non-traditional security activities that Japan was undertaking. Thus, the concept of 'comprehensive security' was adopted and entered into Japanese security practice.[11]

The asymmetry in the US–Japan alliance also shaped Japan's engagement with China during the first half of the Cold War. America's diplomatic recognition of Taiwan (Republic of China) and not the mainland constrained Japan's dealings with China by forcing it to follow suit. In order to circumscribe the constraints where possible, however, Japan made use of its *seikei bunri* policy (separating economics and politics), through which it opened indirect trade relations with China. As a result,

8   Kenneth B Pyle, *The Japanese Question: Power and Purpose in a New Era*, 2nd edn, Washington, DC: AEI Press, 1996, pp. 28–30.
9   Cited in Samuels, *Securing Japan*, 2007, p. 7.
10   Bhubhindar Singh, *Japan's Security Identity: From a Peace State to an International State*, London: Routledge, 2013, p. 56.
11   Kenneth B Pyle, *Japan Rising: The Resurgence of Japanese Power and Purpose*, New York: Public Affairs, 2007, p. 258. On comprehensive security, see Soeya Yoshihide, *Nihon no 'Midoru Pawaa' Gaiko: Sengo Nihon no Sentaku to Koso* (Japan's 'Middle Power' Diplomacy: Postwar Japan's Choices and Conceptions), Tokyo: Chikuma Shinsho, 2005, pp. 153–54.

trade was re-established between the two countries relatively soon after World War II, and indeed was only interrupted subsequently on rare occasions, such as during the outbreak of the Korean War.[12]

When the United States began normalising its diplomatic relations with China in the 1970s, this also allowed Japan to engage China in a more cooperative manner, thereby opening up further trade opportunities for the two countries. From 1978, when it established an economic aid policy for China, Japan actively sought to promote economic development in China based on the reasoning that this was the best way to ensure that China would become a cooperative partner rather than a strategic rival. As Mike Mochizuki points out, 'Japan was using commercial relations and economic aid to encourage a rising neighbour to be benign'.[13] As part of this accommodation, Japan also accepted China's view on the status of Taiwan and agreed to include the 'anti-hegemony' clause (directed at the Soviet Union) in the Peace and Friendship Treaty of 1978.

This is not to suggest, however, that bilateral relations during the period after 1978 were entirely smooth. A dispute over history textbooks in the 1980s led to tensions in Japan's relations not only with China but also with South Korea.[14] Still, as Tsuneo Watanabe points out, Japan's engagement with China during this period was driven by a number of positive developments. These included China's opening up under Deng Xiaoping; the positive nature of Sino-US relations; the complementarity of the growing economies of Japan, China and the United States; and, finally, the optimistic outlook of Japan's political leaders, who sought to deepen economic cooperation through the region, including with China.[15] Overall, Japan's approach to China during this latter part of the Cold War kept within the framework of the US–Japan alliance but was also based around accommodation and avoiding confrontation.

---

12   Linus Hagström, *Japan's China Policy: A Relational Power Analysis*, London: Routledge, 2005, pp. 78–79.
13   Mike M Mochizuki, 'Japan's Shifting Strategy Toward the Rise of China', *Journal of Strategic Studies*, vol. 30, nos 4–5, 2007, p. 747.
14   Claudia Schneider, 'The Japanese History Textbook Controversy in East Asian Perspective', *ANNALS of the American Academy of Political and Social Science*, vol. 617, no. 1, 2008, pp. 109–10. doi.org/10.1177/0002716208314359.
15   Tsuneo Watanabe, 'Japan's Security Strategy toward the Rise of China: From a Friendship Paradigm to a Mix of Engagement and Hedging', Tokyo Foundation, 6 Apr. 2015, viewed Aug. 2016, www.tokyofoundation.org/en/articles/2015/security-strategy-toward-rise-of-china.

Post–Cold War, 1989–2009

The end of the Cold War created tensions in both Japan's alliance policies and its dealings with China. The drawbacks of the Yoshida Doctrine were already being exposed toward the end of the Cold War, and it was soon apparent that the doctrine was not well suited to the emerging post–Cold War order. The Yoshida Doctrine did not offer much direction on how Japan might pursue a more active international role as an advanced economy. At the same time, Americans continued to allege free riding on Japan's part, especially in relation to the 1991 Gulf War, where Japan was disparaged as only delivering 'checkbook diplomacy'.[16]

These failings set off a new political debate in Japan about how the country should approach international politics and the US alliance in the post–Cold War era. This new 'normalisation' debate focused on the idea of becoming a 'normal nation' (*futsū no kuni*), within both the context of the US alliance and wider international relations. It was premised on the idea that Japan's policies during the Cold War, and certainly during the Gulf War, had been abnormal and needed to be changed. Ichirō Ozawa, then in the LDP, argued that Japan had to take on more of the responsibilities of a normal nation and do more to cooperate with others in the international community. Ozawa argued for a strongly globalist vision that loosened the restrictions on Japan's ability to do more on security matters (e.g. peacekeeping), but he also believed that in doing this Japan should be closely tied to international institutions such as the United Nations rather than just the US alliance.[17]

This vision, however, was challenged by international developments in the 1990s and the early 2000s. It failed to provide convincing solutions to emerging instability and security threats in the Asia-Pacific, such as the North Korean nuclear crisis of 1993–94. Instead, this threat, and the subsequent Taiwan Strait crisis, prompted the Japanese Government to work with Washington to restructure the alliance to better deal with the post–Cold War era. As Matake Kamiya explains, the alliance was

---

16   Michael J Green, *Japan's Reluctant Realism: Foreign Policy Challenges in an Era of Uncertain Power*, New York: Palgrave, 2001, p. 17.
17   Ichiro Ozawa, *Blueprint for a New Japan: The Rethinking of a Nation*, Louisa Robinfien (trans.), Eric Gower (ed.), Tokyo: Kodansha International, 1994, pp. 94–95. See also HDP Envall, *Japanese Diplomacy: The Role of Leadership*, Albany, NY: State University of New York Press, 2015, pp. 77–78.

transformed from one intended to 'counter a manifest, specific security threat', such as that provided by the Soviet Union, to one able to address 'latent, unspecified sources of instability'.[18]

It was also undermined by major events elsewhere in the world. In particular, the nuclear tests carried out by India and Pakistan in 1998 exposed Japan's lack of influence in global institutions, and especially the United Nations and, therefore, the assumptions about the utility of these institutions that underpinned the globalists' arguments.[19] Traditional security concerns, such as national defence and the alliance, then returned to the centre of the political agenda following the 9/11 terrorist attacks on the United States in 2001. The Japanese security debates quickly shifted toward alliance cooperation and America's wars in Afghanistan and Iraq.

In place of Ozawa's vision, conservative Japanese politicians, led by Prime Minister Jun'ichirō Koizumi between 2001 and 2006, began implementing a revisionist idea of Japan as a normal nation. This new vision was much more clearly focused on Japan's role in the alliance. In what Richard Samuels describes as 'de facto collective self-defense', Koizumi was able to push Japan toward supporting US activities by passing an anti-terrorism special measures law and dispatching Japanese ships (Aegis destroyers) to the Indian Ocean to support US forces operating in Afghanistan. The Koizumi administration later passed the Iraq Special Measures Law and dispatched Self-Defense Forces to Iraq to undertake humanitarian missions.[20] These actions were part of a wider revision of Japan's security role, with the focus not only on increasing capabilities but also on reforming institutions and changing norms.[21]

Whereas the end of the Cold War brought about considerable change to Japan's alliance policies, the country's approach to China was initially characterised more by continuity, even after the Tiananmen Square

18   Matake Kamiya, 'Reforming the U.S.–Japan Alliance: What Should Be Done?', in G John Ikenberry & Takashi Inoguchi (eds), *Reinventing the Alliance: U.S.–Japan Security Partnership in an Era of Change*, New York: Palgrave Macmillan, 2003, p. 93.
19   Satu Limaye, 'Tokyo's Dynamic Diplomacy: Japan and the Subcontinent's Nuclear Tests', *Contemporary Southeast Asia*, vol. 22, no. 2, 2000, pp. 332–35. doi.org/10.1355/CS22-2E. See also HDP Envall, 'Japan's India Engagement: From Different Worlds to Strategic Partners', in Ian Hall (ed.), *The Engagement of India: Strategies and Responses*, Washington, DC: Georgetown University Press, 2014, pp. 44–46.
20   Samuels, *Securing Japan*, 2007, pp. 94–99. See also Tomohito Shinoda, *Koizumi Diplomacy: Japan's Kantei Approach to Foreign and Defense Affairs*, Seattle, WA: University of Washington Press, 2007, pp. 86–98, 113–32.
21   HDP Envall, 'Transforming Security Politics: Koizumi Jun'ichiro and the Gaullist Tradition in Japan', *Electronic Journal of Contemporary Japanese Studies*, vol. 8, no. 2, art. 3, 2008.

massacre of 1989. Although it imposed sanctions on China in response, the Japanese Government also moved more quickly to a policy of Chinese reintegration. Japan restored its yen loans program to China in 1990 and Emperor Akihito made an historic visit to that country in late 1992.[22] An important outcome of the Tiananmen Square massacre, however, was its effect on popular, as opposed to elite, perceptions of China in Japan. Positive impressions of China amongst the Japanese public fell substantially in this period, from nearly 70 per cent in 1988 to just over 50 per cent following Tiananmen.[23]

Yet, as the 1990s progressed, Japan's approach to China began to change. Japan remained broadly supportive of China's integration into the regional economy, such as by backing its bid to join the World Trade Organization (WTO) in 1999.[24] Political relations, however, deteriorated throughout the decade. The collapse of the Soviet Union, which Japan saw as a major threat through the 1980s, altered the region's basic order. Meanwhile, China's more assertive conduct across Asia, and especially toward Japan over the disputed Senkaku/Diaoyu Islands, began to affect Japanese perceptions of China. Beijing also became more economically and diplomatically active in East Asia, notably by contesting Japanese influence in the region's multilateral institutions, such as the Association of Southeast Asian Nations (ASEAN), and by developing closer bilateral trading relationships around the region.[25] For Japan, the 1993–94 North Korean nuclear crisis created a new sense of insecurity, while China's nuclear tests of 1995 and the Taiwan Strait crisis of 1996 heightened uncertainty regarding China's strategic ambitions. In 1998, Japan was shocked first by a North Korean missile test in August and then by Chinese President Jiang Zemin's strong criticism of Japan's wartime conduct during a state visit in November.[26]

Japan's relations with China worsened through the 2000s, even as economic ties remained strong.[27] That Japan was becoming less tolerant of Chinese criticism regarding its wartime conduct is well illustrated

---

22 Mochizuki, 'Japan's Shifting Strategy toward the Rise of China', 2007, p. 749.

23 Mochizuki, 'Japan's Shifting Strategy toward the Rise of China', 2007, p. 749.

24 Björn Jerdén & Linus Hagström, 'Rethinking Japan's China Policy: Japan as an Accommodator in the Rise of China, 1978–2011', *Journal of East Asian Studies*, vol. 12, no. 2, 2011, p. 232.

25 Mochizuki, 'Japan's Shifting Strategy toward the Rise of China', 2007, pp. 756–57.

26 Reinhard Drifte, *Japan's Security Relations with China since 1989: From Balancing to Bandwagoning?*, London: RoutledgeCurzon, 2003, p. 17.

27 Jerdén & Hagström, 'Rethinking Japan's China Policy', 2011, p. 232.

by Koizumi repeatedly visiting the controversial Yasukuni Shrine (where Japan's war dead, including Class A war criminals, are enshrined). Japan also began to pursue a strategy that involved greater balancing vis-à-vis China, especially by seeking out closer relations with other nations in the region, such as Australia and India.[28] Koizumi's visits to Yasukuni, in turn, created hostility in Beijing (and also in Seoul) toward Japan, with popular anti-Japanese unrest becoming more prevalent throughout China. Tensions also increased as a result of the two sides' ambitions over resource exploration in the East China Sea.[29] Meanwhile, China continued to be more assertive in the region and especially toward Japan. Beijing increased its naval incursions into Japanese territorial waters, such as in 2004, when a Han-class Chinese nuclear submarine passed submerged through Japanese waters.[30]

After Koizumi stepped down in September 2006, the two countries enjoyed a brief period of improving relations—a so-called 'warm spring'.[31] The LDP, under leaders such as Shinzō Abe, sought to improve relations with China, including over history issues as well as earlier resource disputes.[32] When the Democratic Party of Japan (DPJ) came to power in September 2009, it promised a further improvement in bilateral relations. It was especially keen to strengthen Japan's relations in Asia through a proposal for an East Asian Community (EAC). Prime Minister Yukio Hatoyama and Ozawa both favoured a closer relationship with China, although the Chinese did not support the EAC concept. Nevertheless,

28 Derek McDougall, 'Responses to "Rising China" in the East Asian Region: Soft Balancing with Accommodation', *Journal of Contemporary China*, vol. 21, no. 73, 2012, pp. 8–9.

29 On some of the problems over developing resources in the area, see James Manicom, *Bridging Troubled Waters: China, Japan, and Maritime Order in the East China Sea*, Washington, DC: Georgetown University Press, 2014, pp. 145–47. Regarding the anti-Japanese protests, see 'Thousands Join Anti-Japan Protest', *BBC News*, 16 Apr. 2005, viewed Aug. 2016, news.bbc.co.uk/2/hi/asia-pacific/4450975.stm.

30 Manicom, *Bridging Troubled Waters*, 2014, p. 130.

31 Linus Hagström & Björn Jerdén, 'Understanding Fluctuations in Sino–Japanese Relations: To Politicize or to De-politicize the China Issue in the Japanese Diet', *Pacific Affairs*, vol. 83, no. 4, 2010, p. 721. doi.org/10.5509/2010834719.

32 Manicom, *Bridging Troubled Waters*, 2014, pp. 122–65. On Abe's approach to China, see HDP Envall, 'Abe's Fall: Leadership and Expectations in Japanese Politics', *Asian Journal of Political Science*, vol. 19, no. 2, 2011, p. 155. doi.org/10.1080/02185377.2011.600164.

Ozawa took a delegation of DPJ politicians and officials to Beijing in late 2009 to discuss closer relations and to establish better links between the Chinese Communist Party and the DPJ.[33]

The Newly Contested Order, 2009–16

When the revisionism of Koizumi and Abe lost momentum in the late 2000s, the globalism of the 1990s made a comeback in the form of a new 'Asianism'. This was adopted by the DPJ in 2009 and represented a major challenge to the hard-power worldview and US-centrality that revisionists had been attempting to consolidate. With this more Asian-centric approach, the DPJ sought to return Japan to an institutionally focused, comprehensive-security agenda concentrated on integrating Japan more into the region. It also aimed to revise the US–Japan alliance so that Japan would have greater autonomy from the United States— viewed in the wake of the global financial crisis as in decline—and so that the relationship would become more 'equal'. In particular, the DPJ sought to reduce what it saw as an 'alliance burden' on the Japanese public, especially that caused by the presence of US military bases in the country, such as those in the prefecture of Okinawa.[34]

The DPJ's agenda, however, collapsed under the weight of poor leadership, lack of government experience, and an increasingly contested new regional order. In terms of intra-alliance politics, the DPJ struggled to build a functioning relationship with the new US administration under Barack Obama. Hatoyama, in particular, lost the confidence of the United States as he switched between different policies and approaches to the alliance, especially over the Okinawan base issue.[35] The unravelling of the DPJ's alliance policies under Hatoyama caused the DPJ, initially under Naoto

33   HDP Envall & Kiichi Fujiwara, 'Japan's Misfiring Security Hedge: Discovering the Limits of Middle Power Internationalism and "Strategic Convergence"', in William T Tow & Rikki Kersten (eds), *Bilateral Perspectives on Regional Security: Australia, Japan and the Asia-Pacific Region*, Basingstoke: Palgrave Macmillan, 2012, pp. 62–64.

34   Regarding the DPJ's Asianism, see Daniel Sneider, 'The New Asianism: Japanese Foreign Policy under the Democratic Party of Japan', *Asia Policy*, no. 12, 2011, pp. 99–129. See also Envall, 'Clashing Expectations', 2015, pp. 72–73. On the DPJ's Okinawa policy, see HDP Envall & Kerri Ng, 'The Okinawa "Effect" in US–Japan Alliance Politics', *Asian Security*, vol. 11, no. 3, 2015, pp. 231–33. doi.org/10.1080/14799855.2015.1111339.

35   Tomohito Shinoda, *Contemporary Japanese Politics: Institutional Changes and Power Shifts*, New York: Columbia University Press, 2013, pp. 168–79; Masahiro Matsumura, 'Okinawa and the Politics of the Alliance', *Survival*, vol. 53, no. 4, 2011, pp. 157–59. doi.org/10.1080/00396338.201 1.603567.

Kan and then under Yoshihiko Noda, to focus more on the alliance. In late 2010, the government set out its plan to establish a Dynamic Defense Force emphasising greater mobility, versatility and flexibility in the Self-Defense Forces. The plan focused on increasing Japan's capacity to respond effectively to 'grey-zone' conflicts (i.e. disputes that did not automatically constitute war). The DPJ also began engaging in a limited way with the US-backed proposal for a Trans-Pacific Partnership.[36]

These changes did not constitute a transformational agenda in the vein of Koizumi and Abe, but represented an incremental reorientation of Japan's alliance policies. The DPJ refrained from more controversial steps, such as the formal adoption of the right to collective self-defence. Only when the LDP was returned to government in 2012—led once again by Abe—did Japan return to the revisionist agenda. The second Abe administration has subsequently replaced the dynamic defence force idea with the concept of making a 'proactive contribution to peace'. Although euphemistic and vague, this concept is intended to achieve concrete and transformational aims. In its 2013 National Security Strategy, the Abe government envisaged the concept as helping to achieve key national objectives of strengthening the country's deterrence capacity, deepening its alliance with the US, and broadening its regional diplomacy.[37] The accompanying policy changes have encompassed constitutional, institutional and capability adjustments. A National Security Council has been established, the government has 'reinterpreted' the constitution to allow collective self-defence, defence spending has been increased, and a new set of guidelines for US–Japan security cooperation have been adopted.[38]

The Abe administration's strategy, therefore, has been focused on reinforcing the alliance with the United States to ensure that it remains at the centre of Japanese security policy. Japan has been consistently concerned about America's commitment to Japanese security, pushing, for instance, for an explicit understanding that the disputed Senkaku Islands

---

36   Shinoda, *Contemporary Japanese Politics*, 2013, pp. 197–201. See also Envall & Ng, 'The Okinawa "Effect" in US–Japan Alliance Politics', 2015, p. 229.

37   Government of Japan, 'National Security Strategy', 17 Dec. 2013, p. 5.

38   Christopher W Hughes, *Japan's Foreign and Security Policy under the 'Abe Doctrine': New Dynamism or New Dead End?*, Houndmills: Palgrave Macmillan, 2015, pp. 28–69; Jeffrey W Hornung & Mike M Mochizuki, 'Japan: Still An Exceptional U.S. Ally', *Washington Quarterly*, vol. 39, no. 1, 2016, pp. 97–100. On the US–Japan guidelines, see also Tomohiko Satake, 'The New Guidelines for Japan–U.S. Defense Cooperation and an Expanding Japanese Security Role', *Asian Politics and Policy*, vol. 8, no. 1, 2016, pp. 27–38. doi.org/10.1111/aspp.12239.

come under the US–Japan security treaty.[39] Such concerns have also caused Japan to hedge against US abandonment by attempting to forge better relations elsewhere in the Asia-Pacific. It is important, therefore, not to overlook the third of the above objectives: Tokyo's ambition to strengthen the regional dimension of Japanese diplomacy.

Where the DPJ's approach to Asian regionalism was *multilateral*, the LDP under Abe has developed a *minilateral* approach.[40] That is, Tokyo is now attempting to become a more active participant in 'intra-spoke' cooperation with US allies and partners in the region, most notably Australia but also India. This follows on from the approach adopted by Koizumi and Abe to relations with the United States, Australia and India in the early and mid-2000s. Japan is also now seeking to engage more with the nations of South-East Asia, especially the Philippines. In 2012, Abe argued that the United States, Japan, Australia and India should seek to establish a security 'diamond' stretching across the Pacific and Indian oceans to 'safeguard the maritime commons' in the region.[41] Thus far, these types of partnership remain relatively low-key. They are also subject to uncertainty about their trajectory, as illustrated by the recent anxieties in the Japan–Australia strategic partnership over a proposed (but failed) submarine deal.[42] Nevertheless, Japan's increased activity in this area points toward Japan adopting a hybrid approach to security combining alliance reassurance with new forms of regional engagement.[43]

Revival of the Abe agenda did not stem only from the DPJ's poor alliance management. China's rise has stimulated the emergence of a new, more contested regional order that has played an important role

39 Mizuho Aoki, 'Obama Assures Abe on Senkakus', *Japan Times*, 24 Apr. 2014, viewed Aug. 2016, www.japantimes.co.jp/news/2014/04/24/national/obama-tells-abe-security-treaty-covers-senkakus/.
40 HDP Envall, 'Japan's "Pivot" Perspective: Reassurance, Restructuring, and the Rebalance', *Security Challenges*, vol. 12, no. 3, 2016, pp. 17–18.
41 Shinzo Abe, 'Asia's Democratic Security Diamond', *Project Syndicate*, 27 Dec. 2012, viewed Aug. 2016, www.project-syndicate.org/commentary/a-strategic-alliance-for-japan-and-india-by-shinzo-abe.
42 On the Australia–Japan strategic partnership, see Thomas S Wilkins, 'From Strategic Partnership to Strategic Alliance? Australia–Japan Security Ties and the Asia-Pacific', *Asian Policy*, no. 20, 2015, pp. 81–111. Also HDP Envall & Ian Hall, 'Asian Strategic Partnerships: New Practices and Regional Security Governance', *Asian Politics & Policy*, vol. 8, no. 1, 2016, pp. 93–95. doi.org/10.1111/aspp.12241. Regarding the failed Australia–Japan submarine deal specifically, see Nick Bisley & HDP Envall, 'The Morning After: Australia, Japan, and the Submarine Deal that Wasn't', *Asia Pacific Bulletin*, East–West Center, no. 346, 7 Jun. 2016, viewed Aug. 2016, www.eastwestcenter.org/publications/the-morning-after-australia-japan-and-the-submarine-deal-wasn%E2%80%99t.
43 On minilateral engagement, see William T Tow & HDP Envall, 'The U.S. and Implementing Multilateral Security in the Asia-Pacific: Can Convergent Security Work?', *IFANS Review*, vol. 19, no. 1, 2011, pp. 59–60.

in sabotaging the idea of Japan acting 'as a bridge between China and the US'.[44] The 'warm spring' of Sino–Japanese relations that began under Abe, and which Hatoyama had so actively pursued, came to an end in 2010. In March that year, North Korea sank a South Korean corvette (the *Cheonan*); in September a Chinese fishing vessel rammed a Japanese Coast Guard ship near the disputed Senkaku Islands and set off a major diplomatic incident; and, in November, North Korea bombarded the South Korean island of Yeonpyeong. The incident near the Senkaku Islands was particularly damaging to Sino–Japanese relations. China responded to what Japan had initially viewed as a 'policing' issue by demanding compensation and an apology, delaying under mysterious circumstances the export of rare earths to Japan, arresting a number of Japanese in China and increasing its military activity in the East China Sea. This reaction comprehensively undermined the DPJ's Asianist strategy, thereby contributing significantly to the party's return, described earlier, to a more orthodox, alliance-based approach.[45]

In fact, the 2010 incident not only brought about a dip in Sino–Japanese relations, but also led to a more long-term deterioration in mutual threat perceptions. It should be noted that the Japanese Government itself exacerbated matters when, in 2012, Tokyo Governor Shintarō Ishihara, a controversial nationalist, attempted to purchase islands in the Senkaku chain. The DPJ then decided to nationalise all the islands in order to prevent Ishihara from further damaging Sino–Japanese relations. Regardless, China reacted furiously. Violent protests broke out, normal diplomacy was disrupted, and China increased the rate of its naval incursions into the disputed area. Japan, in turn, dispatched coast guard vessels, creating a situation whereby a maritime confrontation between the two nations, although unlikely, was now conceivable.[46] Subsequent incidents, including two in January 2013 where Chinese frigates locked their fire-control radar onto Japanese destroyers in the area, further heightened mutual threat perceptions.[47] By 2014, the mutual disregard

44   Takashi Yokota, 'The Real Yukio Hatoyama; Japan's New Prime Minister Could Be Asia's First "Third Way" Leader', *Newsweek*, 28 Sep. 2009. On the relationship between Hatoyama and Obama, see Tsuyoshi Sunohara, 'The Anatomy of Japan's Shifting Security Orientation', *Washington Quarterly*, vol. 33, no. 4, 2010, pp. 39–57, 51–52.

45   Envall & Fujiwara, 'Japan's Misfiring Security Hedge', pp. 68–71.

46   Thomas U Berger, 'Stormy Seas: Japan–China Clash over Senkakus Hard to Avoid', *Oriental Economist*, vol. 81, no. 1, 2013, pp. 14–16.

47   Itsunori Onodera, 'Extra Press Conference by the Defense Minister', 5 Feb. 2013, viewed Aug. 2016, www.mod.go.jp/e/press/conference/2013/02/05a.html.

had grown to such an extent that Chinese and Japanese diplomats in the United Kingdom were describing each other as the Voldemort (chief villain of the *Harry Potter* books and films) of the Asia-Pacific. This pattern of antagonism, which has continued into 2017—albeit at a lower intensity and with some promising signs of improved communication—has not thus far done major harm to bilateral trade, but is now well established at the heart of the security relationship.[48]

Conclusion: Japan's New Alliance Approach

Japan remains America's most important ally in the Asia-Pacific. Yet, as this chapter demonstrates, Tokyo's view of the alliance, and its role within it, has changed significantly. Perhaps the central shift has been the way in which Japan balances the risks contained in the alliance framework and those presented by the reconfiguration of the regional security environment. This means that the interplay between how Japan sees China's rise and how it seeks its 'secondary alliance dilemma' (the risks of the US–Japan alliance) is reshaping Japan's sense of the part it should play within the alliance.

In terms of regional reconfiguration, although East Asia presents a number of security threats to Japan, such as the North Korean nuclear issue, China's rise is the dominant challenge. This is because China represents both a specific territorial threat and a broader systemic challenge for regional influence. Since the Cold War, as this chapter has outlined, China has increasingly contested Japan on territorial and systemic fronts. Japan's perception of China as both a strategic rival and a direct security threat, therefore, has steadily risen, with Japan now viewing China not through the prism of the post–Cold War order but as the key dynamic in an entirely new, contested order where the regional balance of power is subject to a fresh struggle.

---

48   On the UK exchange, see Liu Xiaoming, 'Liu Xiaoming: China and Britain Won the War Together', *Telegraph*, 1 Jan. 2014, viewed Aug. 2016, www.telegraph.co.uk/comment/10546442/Liu-Xiaoming-China-and-Britain-won-the-war-together.html; Keiichi Hayashi, 'China Risks Becoming Asia's Voldemort', *Telegraph*, 5 Jan. 2014, viewed Aug. 2016, www.telegraph.co.uk/news/worldnews/asia/japan/10552351/China-risks-becoming-Asias-Voldemort.html. For an example of the mutual antagonism from mid-2016, see 'Japan Warned China as Naval Vessel Neared Senkakus, Sources Say', *Japan Times*, 19 Jun. 2016, viewed Aug. 2016, www.japantimes.co.jp/news/2016/06/19/national/japan-warned-china-as-naval-vessel-neared-senkakus-sources-say/.

In the post–Cold War era, Japan adopted a mixed strategy of engagement and soft balancing in an attempt to restrain China's rapid rise while also seeking to integrate China into the established order. As this new, more contested order has emerged, Japan has modified its mixed strategy into one focused more on hard balancing.[49] Since 2010, Tokyo's policy has been to increase the country's hard-power capabilities, strengthening its regional diplomacy, and integrating the country more into the US alliance. Tokyo's experiments with Asian regionalism under the DPJ may, therefore, constitute Japan's last attempt to pursue a strategy based primarily on integrating China into the Asian regional security system. That the DPJ's ambitions were severely damaged by the various incidents in bilateral relations that occurred from 2010 has meant that revisionists, and not globalists, have come to dominate Japan's strategic decision-making.

The revisionists' success has, in turn, reshaped how Japan views its alliance dilemma. Although its perception of alliance risk fluctuated during the Cold War, Japan was chiefly concerned with the dangers of entrapment. In fact, this persisted long after the end of the Cold War. In a new, more contested order, however, abandonment can be expected to become the greater risk. China's rapid rise not only makes it a systemic rival for Japan but also makes balancing Chinese power more challenging. Significantly, this applies not only to Japan but also to the United States, since the superpower now also faces higher potential costs in seeking to balance China. Consequently, Japan's dependence on the United States is increased even as its confidence in the US security guarantee declines. The key question for Tokyo now is whether the US security guarantee, which has been at the heart of the alliance, remains reliable.

By becoming a more active ally, Japan is attempting both to buttress the US position in Asia and to deter China. But the approach has potential risks as well as benefits. On the one hand, Tokyo will likely have less bargaining power in future in terms of resisting pressure from Washington to 'do more' in conflict situations. Accordingly, when making the changes to collective self-defence, the Japanese Government included a number of important restrictions on this new right, not only for domestic political purposes but to retain some capacity to resist outside pressure on Japanese

---

49   Soft balancing here refers to balancing focused on politics or diplomacy, as opposed to hard balancing, which emphasises a military response. See Derek McDougall, 'Responses to "Rising China"', 2012, p. 3.

decision-making. Whether this will prove effective, however, remains to be seen. On the other hand, a more active alliance role may serve a dual purpose for Japan in the coming years. Even as Tokyo's policies are aimed at supporting the United States to stay engaged in the Asia-Pacific, they also create an insurance policy for Japan in case of a US withdrawal from the region. Within Japan's new role as a more active ally, there is the beginning of a hedging strategy that seeks to increase the country's independent deterrence capabilities.

3

Germany: A Lynchpin Ally?

Markus Kaim

At first glance, a chapter on Germany's alliance policy does not seem to call for a title suggesting that Berlin is playing more than a peripheral role in the international system. For most German observers, the notion of Germany as a 'lynchpin ally' is an unusual perspective. For decades the German political class has framed the Bonn and Berlin republics as a sometimes reluctant, sometimes reliable ally within NATO and the European Union, but has never intended to create the perception in other capitals that the future of the Euro–Atlantic security institutions is attached to Germany's military capabilities and the political will to use them. Also, in terms of domestic politics, German politicians have traditionally avoided communicating to their constituency that Germany could or even should play a bigger, more responsible role in international affairs and in multilateral crisis management in particular.

But, due to a variety of factors, things have already changed and will continue to change for the years to come. First, under President Barack Obama, the United States has been prioritising domestic issues and carefully selecting those regional orders and crisis in which to play a more restrained role than previously, thereby leaving a vacuum in terms of sustaining the global international order. Second, the crisis of the European integration process continues with more and more EU regimes falling apart and traditional Europe-shaping powers, like France and the United Kingdom, following an introspective modus operandi. Therefore, in its current form, the European Union cannot fill the vacuum that the United States has left behind. Third, with the annexation of Crimea and the continuing military destabilisation of eastern Ukraine, Russia not only put into question the political and territorial status quo in its neighbourhood, but challenged the norms and principles of the Euro–Atlantic security architecture as laid down, for example, in the 1990 Charter of Paris for a New Europe and following documents. This *acquis*, agreed upon by all member states of the Organization for Security and Cooperation in Europe (OSCE), has been the cornerstone of European (and German) security since the end of the Cold War. These determinants together have, since 2014, triggered a debate in Germany about the changed environment with which German foreign policy is confronted and the more active, more engaged role Berlin has to play within this environment. This debate has just started, but the first shifts, which are probably lasting, are clearly visible now. While this strategic reorientation might not represent Germany as a *transatlantic* lynchpin, it is established as such within the context of Europe and the European Union. This has implications for Germany's foreign policy.

A Different Level of Ambition

A major strategic debate started among German foreign policy elites three years ago. Guided by Chancellor Angela Merkel's foreign policy, this debate was opened by Federal President Joachim Gauck at the Munich Security Conference 2014. In his speech, Gauck pointed to the conflicts that confront Germany and its allies. He called for Germany to have a more active foreign policy:

> For the key question is: has Germany already adequately recognised the new threats and the changes in the structure of the international order? Has it reacted commensurate with its weight? Has Germany shown enough initiative to ensure the future viability of the network of norms, friends and alliances which has brought us peace in freedom and democracy in prosperity? … And, in cases where we have found convincing reasons to join our allies in taking even military action, are we willing to bear our fair share of the risks? Are we doing what we should to attract new and reinvigorated major powers to the cause of creating a just world order for tomorrow? Do we even evince the interest in some parts of the world which is their due, given their importance? What role do we want to

play in the crises afflicting distant parts of the globe? … In my opinion, Germany should make a more substantial contribution, and it should make it earlier and more decisively if it is to be a good partner.[1]

Foreign Minister Frank-Walter Steinmeier and Minister of Defence Ursula von der Leyen made similar points in their speeches at the same conference.[2] Taken together, these speeches mark a notable shift in Germany's approach to its foreign policy since 2014. In many ways, Germany is the locus point of EU foreign policymaking. During a time plagued by wars and conflict, Merkel managed to show leadership while also integrating other EU countries into a specifically German approach. That was no mean feat for a country so often criticised for not taking on responsibility commensurate with its size and economic power. If anything, the foreign policy ambition of Merkel's third government is remarkable. It is definitely higher than that of her previous coalition, which wouldn't be difficult given the government's lacklustre approach in this field. It's not that Germany didn't use its weight under the first two Merkel governments. Ask anyone in Greece whether they think that Berlin was unaware of its power as it insisted on tough austerity measures for the single currency area. But Germany's weight and influence were mainly geared toward just that—economic and structural reform in the Eurozone—rather than toward foreign policy issues.

This balance changed with the Ukraine crisis. When Russia began meddling in Ukraine, Merkel proved her critics wrong. Those critics claimed that her interests in foreign affairs and international security policy were limited. Indeed, it is Merkel who has been engaged in crisis management efforts, and engaged with Russian President Vladimir Putin, as delegated by Obama. At the same time, Merkel and Steinmeier coordinated the EU approach toward Moscow and, despite immense differences among the 28 member states over Russia, have maintained European unity on the sanctions imposed against Moscow.

1   Joachim Gauck, 'Germany's Role in the World: Reflections on Responsibility, Norms and Alliances', speech at the opening of the Munich Security Conference, 31 Jan. 2014, www.bundespraesident.de/SharedDocs/Downloads/DE/Reden/2014/01/140131-Muenchner-Sicherheitskonferenz-Englisch.pdf?__blob=publicationFile. See also Alison Smale, 'Spurred by Global Crises, Germany Weighs a More Muscular Foreign Policy', *New York Times*, 1 Feb. 2014.
2   'Speech by the Federal Minister of Defense, Dr. Ursula von der Leyen, on the Occasion of the 50th Munich Security Conference Munich, 31 January 2014', www.securityconference.de/fileadmin/MSC_/2014/Reden/2014-01-31-Speech-MinDef_von_der_Leyen-MuSeCo.pdf.

But the concern for Germany goes further than Crimea or the EU's European Neighbourhood Policy. More clearly than many other observers, Merkel has understood that there is a linkage between the Ukraine crisis and the German ability to shape and influence the world. Since 1949, German policy has been based on the existence of effective international organisations and established norms and principles rather than on military capabilities. In this respect, German engagement in the Ukraine crisis is not only about helping others; the Russian-induced erosion of the Euro–Atlantic security order directly affects Berlin's capability to shape and influence international affairs. The government's decision to apply for the OSCE chairmanship in 2016 reflects these considerations and the increased will to shoulder more responsibility in the global arena.[3] Another example is Berlin's interest in running for a rotating seat in the UN Security Council in the years 2019/2020.

It's not only the Ukraine crisis that has preoccupied the Merkel government in recent years. One of Germany's more strategic diplomatic endeavours has been its leading role in negotiations with Tehran on Iran's nuclear program. This role should not be underestimated. Berlin initiated the talks together with Paris and London back in 2003 and was a driving force behind them until the agreement on the Joint Comprehensive Plan of Action in July 2015. This strong engagement is consistent with Germany's commitment to the security of Israel, its general interest in furthering arms control, and its firm economic and political relationship with Tehran. Being a key trading partner of Iran certainly furthered Germany's interest in finding a diplomatic solution to the dispute over Iran's nuclear program.

More recently, the worsening situation in Syria has spurred the Merkel government to adopt a more active, multipronged approach to this part of the region. This includes the acceptance of more than 200,000 Syrian refugees into Germany (not including the additional number of Syrian asylum seekers, whose applications have not been decided yet), support for trans-border humanitarian support into Syria, and increased efforts by the German security services to monitor and stem the flow of foreign fighters from Germany to Syria and Iraq. In an unexpected turn,

---

3   Federal Foreign Office, 'Renewing Dialogue, Rebuilding Trust, Restoring Security. The Priorities of the German OSCE Chairmanship in 2016', www.osce.org/cio/215791?download=true. See also Hanns W. Maull, 'What German Responsibility Means', *Security and Human Rights*, vol. 26, no. 1, 2015, pp. 11–24. doi.org/10.1163/18750230-02601012.

Berlin also decided in the summer of 2014 to provide arms and training to the Kurdish Peshmerga forces to help contain the expansion of the so-called Islamic State of Iraq and Syria (ISIS). In December 2015, a large majority of the German Bundestag voted in favour of the deployment of up to 1,200 troops (according to the mandate—the actual number is 268 as of 8 May 2017) to reinforce the international alliance against ISIS, following the 13 November Paris terrorist attacks. This led Germany to provide support in the form of reconnaissance and logistics as well as protection components. In addition to satellite reconnaissance, Tornado jets have been deployed to help obtain a precise picture of the situation on the ground. Over and above this, Germany has provided an aerial refuelling plane, a frigate to escort a French aircraft carrier and staff unit and headquarters staff. While these decisions reflect Germany building its influence in a regional conflict, there is still continued reluctance from the German Government to engage German armed forces in any large-scale combat operation. And, even more importantly, this support lacks the necessary strategic underpinning: the military as well as the political goal remain undefined and rather unclear.

This more ambitious, more engaged German foreign and security policy approach of the last two years has gone hand in hand with a parallel intellectual effort to provide a sober analysis of Germany's changed security environment, and the role Germany should play in it, as encouraged and requested by Gauck in Munich three years ago. Importantly it should come as no surprise that the decision to draft two major strategic documents date back to 2014, because the recent crises revealed an ongoing lack of a durable and coherent strategic orientation for German foreign policy.[4]

In February 2014, the German Foreign Office launched a public discussion process by introducing the project *Review 2014: A Fresh Look at Foreign Policy*, which posed two deliberately provocative questions to experts in Germany and abroad: What, if anything, is wrong with German foreign policy? What needs to be changed? The overarching aim of the review was to conduct a process of reflection on German foreign policy's future prospects by way of dialogue between the federal Foreign Office and the most important foreign and security policy stakeholders, including civil society. In February 2015, Steinmeier presented the final report *Crisis –*

---

4   Adrian GV Hyde-Price, 'The "Sleep-Walking Giant" Awakes: Resetting German Foreign and Security Policy', *European Security*, vol. 24, no. 4, 2015, p. 605.

Order – Europe to the German Bundestag and the public.[5] It encapsulated the three phases of the review process, including discussion with experts from Germany and abroad, and talks with federal Foreign Office staff. The conclusion was that, as the world changes, so should German foreign policy. Germany's medium-term foreign policy challenges included crisis prevention, crisis management and post-crisis support; shaping the elements of a new global order; and embedding German foreign policy even more firmly in Europe.

Germany's need for strategic reflection and orientation is also illustrated by von der Leyen's decision to define the country's security policy priorities in a new defence white paper, *White Paper on German Security Policy and the Future of the Bundeswehr*.[6] In the previous white paper—published in 2006—Germany's security policies were mostly attuned to Afghanistan. Russia was defined as a partner, and the Arab Spring and the emergence of ISIS terrorist militia were still in the distant future. Now German politicians are facing a different environment: war rages in Ukraine, Russia and NATO members eye one another like they did when the Iron Curtain still stood, and Germany is actively participating in the fight against ISIS. Two guidelines seem to be certain: first, it has emphasised Germany's self-perception as a middle power in international affairs with aspirations to shape the world together with European and transatlantic partners, thereby striking a different tone compared to the widespread isolationist, anti-integrationist and anti-globalist mood in France and the United Kingdom. Second, the white paper prioritises Germany's level of ambition. Although the country is highly globalised and affected by global events like only a few others, its foreign policy ambition is not global. Instead, German security policy will focus for the years to come on crisis management in the neighbourhood of the European Union.

The Political–Societal Background

Germany's foreign policy does not reflect the mood of the constituency. In spring 2014, Germany's leading electoral and political research institute, TNS Infratest, conducted a survey to gauge the public's general

5   For the final report, see *Review 2014: A Fresh Look at Foreign Policy*, Berlin: Federal Foreign Office, 2014.
6   See *White Paper on German Security Policy and the Future of the Bundeswehr 2016*, Berlin: Federal Ministry of Defence, 2016.

approach to foreign and security policy. While there was widespread interest in foreign policy issues, there is only lukewarm support for greater international involvement: 60 per cent believe that Germany should continue to exercise restraint in the area of foreign policy, whereas 37 per cent are in favour of greater German involvement. The positions have changed dramatically compared to attitudes in 1994: 37 per cent were in favour of German restraint, whereas 62 per cent were in favour of assuming greater responsibility.[7] Asked about the reasons for their opinion, 73 per cent of the respondents state that the main reason why they are in favour of greater restraint is that Germany has enough problems of its own, and that it should try to resolve them before dealing with other issues. And 50 per cent justified their reticence by referring to German history, a stance that tends to be taken in particular by respondents over 60 years of age; 37 per cent believe that Germany's influence in the world is too small to make much of a difference. Taken together, public opinion in Germany shows the same 'introspective mode', which can be observed in the United States and a lot of European countries.

The 37 per cent who are in favour of greater involvement adduce the following arguments in support of their views: Germany owes its economic prosperity to international trade and should thus make a contribution to world peace and global security (93 per cent); Germany's greater political and economic significance should be reflected in the assumption of more international responsibility (89 per cent); and Germany is globally respected as a mediator (85 per cent).

When asked more specifically about the use of military force, public opinion gives a rather traditional response: 82 per cent of respondents were in favour of cutting back on German military missions. This attitude was reflected in all age groups, and was particularly noticeable for those over the age of 60 (90 per cent). A small majority rejected support for other countries in armed conflicts without direct German military participation, and a clear majority were even against arms deliveries to allied countries. Respondents would support intervention by German armed forces only if peace and security in Europe were directly threatened, for humanitarian purposes, in the case of a direct threat to Germany's allies, in the context of peacekeeping measures based on international agreements, and in order to prevent genocide and the spread of weapons of mass destruction.

---

7   *Involvement or Restraint? Findings of a Representative Survey Conducted by TNS Infratest Policy Research on German Attitudes to Foreign Policy*, Hamburg: Körber Foundation, May 2014, p. 2.

Although the protection of human rights is considered to be the most important task of German foreign policy, and genocide an important reason for military intervention, a majority of Germans (66 per cent) are not prepared to give their blessing to a military mission for humanitarian reasons without the requisite UN mandate. Only 33 per cent would support intervention for humanitarian reasons in the absence of an appropriate mandate from the UN Security Council. Regardless of the multilateral framework in which German expeditionary missions might take place (United Nations, NATO, European Union), the decision to deploy German armed forces or even to use military force remains a contentious issue in Berlin, to address which requires a lot of political capital to be invested by the political class.

Multilateral Crisis Management

Since the normalisation of German foreign policy in the post–Cold War era, one narrative has guided all German governments regardless of political orientation: although the prime purpose of NATO traditionally has been collective defence, the changed security environment after 1990, with its plethora of diverse security challenges, has made this task largely irrelevant. Due to several rounds of NATO and EU enlargement and the lack of a serious threat to Euro–Atlantic security, Germany would be encircled by a ring of friends and the ongoing success of the European integration process would perpetuate Germany's stability and security. Smaller armed forces and a decreasing defence budget could not only be possible, but also a strategic choice as a welcome peace dividend and contribution to a more peaceful world.

The only remaining circumstances in which the use of military force could be legitimised has been the deployment of the German armed forces for collective defence, mandated by the UN Security Council and conducted within a multilateral framework. And, in this case, Germany has come a long way. Berlin has contributed to an array of military operations over a wide geographical area since the beginning of the 1990s including UN peacekeeping in Cambodia and Somalia, peace support operations in the Balkans, humanitarian military intervention in Kosovo, counterterrorism and counterinsurgency in Afghanistan, Common Security and Defence Policy missions in Africa and maritime security operations in the Mediterranean and off the Horn of Africa.

Until the crisis years, and even today, Germany's military engagement has focused on collective security. It is the driver behind the largest and longest engagements of the German armed forces. By January 2017, 880 German soldiers were participating in the NATO-led Resolute Support Mission (RSM), the follow-up to the International Security Assistance Force mission, which brought the first German soldiers to Afghanistan in 2001 and ended on 31 December 2014. They continue to help train, advise and assist the Afghan security forces without participating in combat. In Kosovo, more than 500 soldiers are still deployed as part of the Kosovo Force (KFOR), the NATO-led international peacekeeping force that has been responsible for establishing a secure environment in Kosovo since 1999. After the end of the immediate hostilities between Serb and Kosovo Albanians, KFOR today focuses on contributing to a safe and secure environment, coordinating the international humanitarian efforts, facilitating the development of a stable, democratic, multiethnic and peaceful Kosovo, and supporting the development of the Kosovo Security Force. More than 150 German soldiers participate in the two EU-led maritime missions: 120 have been deployed within the framework of the European Union Naval Force—Mediterranean, which aims to undertake systematic efforts to identify, capture and dispose of vessels to fight human smugglers and traffickers due to the human emergency in the Mediterranean Sea. Roughly 30 of them continue to contribute to the European Union Naval Force—Operation Atalanta. As a reaction to the expansion of Somali-based piracy and armed robbery at sea off the Horn of Africa and in the western Indian Ocean, and its impact on international trade and maritime security and on the economic activities and security of countries in the region, the European Union protects vessels of the UN World Food Programme, the African Union Mission in Somalia and other vulnerable shipping since December 2008. At the same time, it deters and disrupts piracy as well as armed robbery at sea and monitors fishing activities off the coast of Somalia.

The most recent decisions of the German Bundestag to deploy up to 1,200 soldiers to Syria and, in January 2017, 1,000 soldiers to the Multidimensional Integrated Stabilization Mission in Mali (MINUSMA) operation follow exactly the same paradigm: that Germany can and should strengthen the UN system of collective security regardless of the multilateral organisation through which these operations are conducted.[8]

---

8 'Germany to Deploy Helicopters, More soldiers to UN Mission in Mali', *Reuters*, 11 Jan 2017, www.reuters.com/article/us-mali-un-germany-idUSKBN14V131.

From Security Provider to Security Consultant

Given the widespread disillusionment in the political class as well as the broader public about what has been accomplished with German military engagements in the past, for example, in Afghanistan, the Merkel government has made it clear that Germany wants to take on more responsibility in foreign policy but is keen, as far as possible, to avoid direct military involvement in the future. Confronted with a rising number of crises in Europe, Merkel has advocated a subsidiary policy to support other countries and regional organisations in providing security and stability in their respective environments. Providing training and equipment for governments and regional organisations in crisis areas enables them to create and maintain peace and security by their own efforts, Hence, Germany was one of the driving forces of the December 2013 European Council meeting of EU leaders, which emphasised the importance of empowering global partners to take more responsibility for regional security.

The concept of capacity-building—providing advice, training and equipment to strengthen partners' own capabilities—has featured on Germany's foreign policy agenda for some years now, albeit mostly in the context of broader crisis prevention and management efforts. One priority in this regard has been Germany's engagement in Mali. The restoration of security and lasting peace in Mali is a major issue for the stability of the Sahel region, as well as Africa and Europe more broadly. In February 2013, at the request of the Malian authorities, the European Union launched EU Training Mission Mali, a training mission for Malian armed forces. For this purpose, roughly 130 German soldiers have been deployed to the West African country. The aim of the mission is to support the rebuilding of the Malian armed forces and to meet their operational needs by providing expertise and advice, in particular as regards operational and organic command, logistic support, human resources, operational preparation and intelligence. The mission is not involved in combat operations. The EU Training Mission Somalia (with 10 German soldiers) follows more or less the same approach.

While a controversial mission, since the beginning of 2015 more than 150 Bundeswehr soldiers have participated in a training mission for Iraqi armed forces and Kurdish Peshmerga fighters in northern Iraq.

The context for this mission is the developments since summer 2014, when ISIS started its military advances in Iraq and Syria. Many people were killed and hundreds of thousands were forced to flee their homes. Germany has also responded to an earlier request from the Iraqi side and Kurdish–Iraqi forces and gave its approval for the Peshmerga fighters to be supported through the provision of military equipment and weapons. Germany is providing this help within the framework of the international alliance against terror, which comprises more than 60 countries and provides military and humanitarian aid in the fight against ISIS.

Together with a handful of smaller contingents, the German armed forces have currently (2,500 as of 8 May 2017) deployed 2,900 soldiers for different kinds of out-of-area operations.

The Return of Collective Defence

Even before the Ukraine/Russia crisis, the focus of NATO was shifting away from large-scale stabilising operations. One explanation for this is that decision-makers have been realistic about the political constraints they face, realising that stabilisation operations cannot be the core tasks of NATO. Instead, the focus has been on a gradual reduction of global military engagements and on preserving interoperability activities, as seen in Kosovo, Libya and Afghanistan. This policy has been illustrated by the efforts of NATO's Connected Forces Initiative (CFI) of 2012, an attempt designed to increase allied interoperability. Through three lines of effort—training and education, exercises and better use of technology—the CFI was designed to help the alliance maintain the tremendous level of operational and tactical interoperability it has developed in the years before.[9]

In this respect, the Ukraine crisis has only accelerated an already existing development. Collective defence as NATO's prime purpose has, however, been 'rediscovered' by the German political class and the wider public due to the revisionist Russian foreign policy under Putin, and the growing fear among Central and Eastern European NATO countries that they could also be confronted with growing political pressure, territorial ambitions

---

9   Stephen J Maranian, *NATO Interoperability, Sustaining Trust and Capacity within the Alliance*, Research Paper no. 115, Rome: NATO Defense College, 2015.

and forms of hybrid warfare.[10] That does not mean that Russia is perceived as a permanent threat to Germany's security. On the contrary, Russian foreign policy enjoys an understanding in Germany like in no other Western country. But the decision to contribute to reassurance measures for Eastern neighbours is driven by two strategic considerations. First, their security concerns will not be alleviated by vague rhetorical assurance of alliance solidarity, but only by a credible NATO military posture (with a clear German footprint). Otherwise the alliance's credibility would be weakened, its commitments hollow and, at the end of the day, the Central Eastern European NATO members might look somewhere else to protect their political sovereignty and territorial integrity. Second, an unequivocal German commitment to the protection of those countries gives Berlin the necessary leverage to influence their foreign policy behaviour and to avoid any unwanted escalation in the relationship between NATO and Russia. In this respect, military reassurance and the de-escalation of the conflict as well as the exploration of all diplomatic avenues for a political solution are, in the eyes of the Merkel government, two sides of the same coin.

In response to the Ukraine crisis, NATO allies decided at the September 2014 summit in Wales on the most fundamental military evolution of the alliance since the end of the Cold War. The objective was a large-scale reinforcement and reorganisation of defence capabilities, requiring considerable political, military and financial input from all allies. Additional measures were adopted at the 2016 Warsaw summit that are intended to ensure credible deterrence. These include establishment, on a rotational basis, battalion-sized force contingents in each of the three Baltic states, as well as in Poland.

Berlin played a considerable part in shaping the Wales decisions and the partners continue to expect Germany to bear a substantial military and financial burden because of its economic strength. With regard to assurance measures, Germany has, for instance, increased its naval participation in the Baltic Sea and is sending significantly more soldiers on NATO exercises. As for the agreed adaptation measures, Germany has been the first state to take on the command of the new Very High Readiness Joint Task Force (VJTF) in 2015.[11] The Multinational Corps

---

10   Heidi Reisinger & Aleksandr Golts, *Russia's Hybrid Warfare. Waging War below the Radar of Traditional Collective Defence*, Research Paper no. 105, Rome: NATO Defense College, 2014.

11   Jan Abts, *NATO's Very High Readiness Joint Task Force. Can the VJTF Give New Elan to the NATO Response Force?*, Research Paper no. 109, Rome: NATO Defense College, 2015.

North-East, which Germany, Poland and Denmark are jointly running in Stettin, Poland, will increase its readiness, take on more tasks and will become a hub for regional cooperation. Most strikingly, Berlin recently announced its willingness to serve as a 'framework nation' on the Eastern flank of the alliance, promising to lead a multinational battalion in Lithuania as part of NATO's Enhanced Forward Presence.[12] In overview it turns out that, among the European NATO members, Germany is providing the backbone for the successful implementation of the Wales and Warsaw decisions. Without Berlin's participation, they would be hardly feasible.[13]

Conclusion

With regard to political will, it has been become evident that the Merkel government since 2014 has had a higher level of ambition in foreign and security policy than in the years before. This can be explained to a certain degree by different personnel in key ministries, but also— and even more importantly—by the changed power structure of the international system and higher expectations of Germany from its traditional allies within the European Union and NATO. As long as the United States and major powers within the European Union continue to be preoccupied with domestic priorities, Germany cannot escape the role of a Führungsmacht (leading power). In the German context, leading always means 'in a European context' and 'together with others'— however, German foreign and security officials do not deny any more that the Merkel government has the political will to influence European and international security.[14] At least two caveats come into play, however. First, Berlin does not pretend to be a global power. Instead priority will be given to crisis management in the European periphery to the east (the ongoing Russia–Ukraine crisis), to the south-east (the advancement of ISIS in

---

12   Diego A Ruiz Palmer, *The Framework Nations' Concept and NATO: Game-Changer for a New Strategic Era or Missed Opportunity?*, Research Paper no. 132, Rome: NATO Defense College, 2016.
13   Rainer L Glatz & Martin Zapfe, *NATO Defence Planning between Wales and Warsaw. Politico-military Challenges of a Credible Assurance against Russia*, SWP Comments no. 5/16, Berlin 2016.
14   Here the author disagrees with Sten Rynning's assessment that '[t]he sum total is a Germany which seeks to inspire confidence abroad, which invites cooperation, but which is ill prepared to take a leading role. Germany is peaceful but insular in this sense' (*Germany is More Than Europe Can Handle: Or, Why NATO Remains a Pacifier*, Research Paper no. 96, Rome: NATO Defense College, 2013, p. 5). See also Franz-Josef Meiers, 'The Stress Test of German Leadership', *Survival*, vol. 57, no. 2, 2015, pp. 47–55. doi.org/10.1080/00396338.2015.1026061.

Syria and Iraq) and the south (the fragile situation in North Africa after the revolutionary wave of 2011). Second, the current German strength has a lot to do with the temporary weakness of others. A more ambitious and engaged French president might change the power equation. In this respect, Berlin's central political role will be temporary. But, as long as things stand as they are, Germany is a lynchpin ally, maybe less within a transatlantic context, but definitely for and among Europeans.

4

Continuity Amidst Change:
The Korea – United States Alliance

Youngshik Bong

The Republic of Korea (RoK) – United States alliance dates from the signing of the Mutual Defence Treaty on 1 October 1953. Its signing— just two months after the conclusion of an armistice agreement—brought the Korean War to a halt, and its provisions—allowing the permanent stationing of foreign troops in an intensely nationalistic country that had endured decades of colonial occupation—underpins the central role the United States had come to play in South Korean security. The southern part of the Korean Peninsula was administered by an American military government from the end of World War II, and it was in the months following the withdrawal of US forces in 1949 that North Korea chose to make its devastating attack on the South. Seventy years later, with almost every other factor in North-East Asia having been transformed, it is South Korea's pervasive sense of insecurity that maintains the strength of the alliance, despite a range of complicating factors.

As a security commitment, the RoK–US alliance is much less equivocal than other US alliances in Asia. The operative clause of the RoK–US Mutual Defence Treaty states that if either party is attacked by a third country, the other will act to meet the common danger. The United States maintains 28,500 troops in South Korea and these, along with the 650,000-strong RoK armed forces, are closely integrated in command and communications, and both Korean and American forces will be under US command in wartime. Despite the alliance's main focus on the Korean

45

Peninsula, it has long had an extra-regional dimension. South Korea committed over 300,000 troops to the Vietnam War, the second-largest expeditionary contingent after the United States; and, more recently, Seoul sent 3,000 non-combat troops to Iraq and 300 non-combat troops to Afghanistan.

Despite these elements of integration, there is a range of complicating factors in the alliance, and it is the management of these complicating factors that shapes the central alliance dynamics. This chapter will review four key complicating factors in the alliance—North Korea, the rise of China, alliance asymmetries, and changing role conceptions—in order to illustrate some of the key challenges and responses in managing the RoK–US alliance.

Handling North Korea

North Korea's aggression and unpredictability have consistently provided the basis for the alignment of strategic interests that has underpinned the RoK–US alliance but, at the same time, they have created some of the most damaging friction between Washington and Seoul. By one count, between 1953 and 2003, North Korea was responsible for 1,439 major security 'provocations' and for the deaths of 390 RoK and 90 US soldiers.[1] Since the early 1990s, the threat from North Korea has become even greater due to Pyongyang's development of nuclear weapons technology, its willingness to engage in direct aggression against the South, and the advent of a third-generation Kim dynasty leader who is younger and seemingly more ruthless than his father and grandfather. North Korea is believed to have around 40 kilograms of plutonium, enough to build around 12 nuclear devices, although there are differing views about how capable it is of miniaturising these for installation on ballistic missiles. Since 2008, Pyongyang has tested nuclear devices in October 2006, May 2009, February 2013, January 2016 and September 2016; tested ballistic missiles in April 2009, April 2012, December 2012, February 2016, October 2016 and February–June 2017; attacked and sunk the RoK naval vessel *Cheonan* in March 2010; shelled the South Korean island Yeonpyeong-do in November 2010; and detonated a landmine on the southern side of the demilitarised zone in August 2015.

1   Leon Whyte, 'The Evolution of the US–South Korea Alliance', *The Diplomat*, 13 Jun. 2015.

During the Cold War, Seoul and Washington had a closely coordinated approach to the North Korean issue. The problem of the Democratic People's Republic of Korea (DPRK) was seen as an extension of the strategy of containment, with US forces in South Korea playing much the same 'tripwire' role as they were in continental Europe. The end of the Cold War brought real differences between Seoul and Washington over North Korea to the surface. While in Washington there was an expectation that the Cold War's end would bring about a relatively unproblematic unification of the two Koreas, much as had happened between the two Germanys, South Korean hopes were tinged with more than a little apprehension. The first real test of the alliance over North Korea came during the 1993–94 first North Korean nuclear crisis, during which Washington and Seoul coordinated their actions well. Real cracks opened up, however, during the second North Korean nuclear crisis in 2002, which, according to David Kang, 'showed how far the two countries had drifted apart in their foreign policies and perceptions'.[2]

The 2002 North Korean nuclear crisis showed that a decade of perseverance rather than collapse by the DPRK had opened up divisions between South Korea and the United States about how best to handle North Korea. Seoul had become concerned more about the DPRK's chaotic collapse than about its nuclear or conventional aggression, and had embarked on a policy of transformation of North Korea through engagement. Successive RoK presidents pursued dialogue with the North and supported the development of the Kaesong Industrial Complex, which saw the location of South Korean industry in a North Korean industrial zone, as a path towards economic and hopefully political transformation. The United States, however, continued to view North Korea through the lenses of military aggression, authoritarianism and nuclear proliferation, and became wedded to a program of regime transformation. Most concerning to many South Korean policymakers was that many of their counterparts in Washington, particularly in the administration of President George W Bush, seemed unconcerned about whether North Korea underwent a 'hard' or a 'soft' collapse.

---

2   David C Kang, 'Rising Powers, Offshore Balancers, and Why the US–Korea Alliance is Undergoing Strain', *International Journal of Korean Unification Studies*, vol. 14, no. 2, 2005, p. 116.

During this period, and particularly in the context of the Six-Party Talks, China emerged as an alternative significant actor in relation to the problem of North Korea.[3] As Pyongyang became ever more unpredictable, it became clear that Beijing was the only player able to wield carrots and sticks to try to influence North Korea's behaviour. Furthermore, it became ever more obvious to Seoul that Beijing's interests in relation to North Korea were much closer to its own than Washington's were. Whereas Beijing prioritised stability and behavioural change, Washington prioritised confrontation, isolation and coercion. There was a growing sentiment among South Korean policymakers that China was a stabilising and influential player on the Korean Peninsula, while Washington was destabilising, decreasingly influential and liable to undo years of Seoul's compromise and hard work in engaging and socialising North Korea.[4]

A new round of North Korean unpredictability and aggression unleashed dynamics that moderated these tensions. Perhaps alarmed by the growing closeness of Sino-RoK relations, North Korea's torpedoing of the *Cheonan* and shelling of Yeonpyeong-do opened up a rift between Seoul and Beijing. South Koreans were angered by China's ambivalence over attributing the sinking of the *Cheonan*, at the cost of 40 South Korean lives, to North Korea—despite the unequivocal judgement from an international panel of experts that North Korea was responsible. Later that year, South Koreans' anger towards China deepened when Beijing was also ambivalent about condemning Pyongyang over the shelling of Yeonpyeong-do. Subsequent toughness from Beijing towards North Korea over its nuclear and ballistic missile tests has failed to mollify many in South Korea, particularly among conservatives, who now doubt China's trustworthiness on North Korea. The conservative administration of President Park Geun-hye gradually abandoned the conciliatory aspects of its 'trustpolitik' approach to the North, in favour of increasing pressure on Pyongyang through measures such as closing the Kaesong Industrial Complex after the North's fourth nuclear test in 2016.

The new phase of North Korean aggressiveness coincided with a new president in the White House, who has shown a real willingness for the United States to follow Seoul's lead on dealing with North Korea.

3   Leszek Buszynski, *Negotiating with North Korea: The Six Party Talks and the Nuclear Issue*, London: Routledge, 2013, pp. 78–110.
4   Ted Galen Carpenter & Douglas Bandow, *The Korean Conundrum: America's Troubled Relations with North and South Korea*, London: Palgrave Macmillan, 2004.

Pyongyang's aggression, and the new US approach has ushered in essentially a joint approach to dealing with North Korea, which has four main aspects: keeping the door open to restarting six-party talks on the condition that Pyongyang takes 'irreversible steps' towards denuclearisation, insisting that any six-party or US–DPRK talks must be preceded by North–South Korea talks and improvements in relations, trying to gradually alter China's strategic assessment of North Korea, and responding strongly to Pyongyang's provocations by tightening sanctions and conducting beefed-up military exercises.[5] The closeness of the RoK and American positions has also been reflected in a pragmatic revision of the Korean forces' rules of engagement in the advent of another North Korean conventional attack—a revision that was seen to be necessary after RoK forces were constrained by the terms of the alliance from responding more forcefully after the November 2010 shelling of Yeonpyeong-do.

The oscillation in RoK–US alliance relations with respect to North Korea reflects some key underlying realities in the alliance. The key independent variables affecting the allies' closeness on this issue appear to have been the political alignment of the South Korean administration and its policy approach to North Korea, the level of provocation undertaken by Pyongyang, and the prevailing global approach in US foreign policy at the time. All of these issues are of course highly changeable, and there is little within the alliance that suggests that, should each of these factors change—and importantly align, a new period of estrangement within the alliance could develop.

The Rise of China

As David Kang notes, South Korea appears to be the only US ally or partner in Asia not to have engaged in either external or internal balancing behaviour against the rise of China.[6] Unlike most other countries in the region, South Korea has not significantly upgraded its security cooperation with the United States or other regional states since the mid-1990s, and its arms spending has been falling even as China's has been growing strongly. Despite China's geographic proximity and increasingly assertive behaviour

5   Mark E Manyin, Emma Chanlett-Avery, Mary Beth D Nikitin, Ian E Rinehart & Brock R Williams, *US–South Korean Relations*, Congressional Research Service Report 7–5700, 26 Apr. 2016, p. 13.
6   Kang, 'Rising Powers, Offshore Balancers', 2005, p. 30.

in the East and South China Seas, there is no evidence that South Koreans consider it to be a rising threat—in clear contrast to a significant number of publics in other regional countries.

Part of the explanation lies in the remarkable growth of economic relations between South Korea and China over the past quarter-century. Currently, over one-fifth of South Korea's total trade is with China, larger than South Korea's trade with both Japan and the United States combined. South Korean industry has eagerly invested in China as well, making China the number one location for Korean FDI, and becoming the largest single source of foreign investment in China. These trade and investment linkages have only accelerated since the signing of the China–RoK Free Trade Agreement in 2015. As in the security realm, there is no clear evidence that South Koreans see China as an economic threat—although Seoul has been signing FTAs with a range of outside countries and has indicated a strong interest in joining the Trans-Pacific Partnership.

Another element bringing greater closeness between Seoul and Beijing has been a shared concern about Japan's security 'normalisation'. South Korea and China are the two countries in the region most sensitive about Japan's past war crimes, and Tokyo's perceived unwillingness to adequately acknowledge and atone for its past behaviours. Both countries are most prone to outbreaks of anti-Japanese nationalism when issues of Japan's past come to prominence. Added to this, both countries have outstanding and emotionally charged territorial disputes with Japan. As discussed above, there are many South Koreans who have favoured China's approach to dealing with the North Korean issue over that of the United States.

American strategists have worried for over a decade about the growing warmth of Sino-RoK ties, which has prompted them to ask whether South Korea will be the first ally to leave the US alliance system and gravitate towards bandwagoning with a rising China.[7] These feelings were particularly stirred during the administration of President Roh Moo-hyun but somewhat quietened during the conservative administration of President Lee Myung-bak. President Park began her term in office developing a strong rapport with the Chinese leadership, holding six summit meetings with Chinese president Xi Jinping during her first three years in office.

---

7   Victor D Cha, 'Korea: A Peninsula in Crisis and Flux', in Ashley J Tellis & Michael Wills (eds), *Strategic Asia 2004–5: Confronting Terrorism in the Pursuit of Power*, Seattle: NBR, 2004.

There have not, however, been uniformly positive developments in South Korean–Chinese relations. In 2004, South Koreans were shocked and angered when Chinese media and government statements claimed the ancient Koguryo kingdom (73 BCE – 688 CE) to have been Chinese. Koguryo is central to the modern Korean sense of identity and, when Beijing refused to back down on the claim, opinion polls found that the number of South Koreans believing China to be the RoK's most important diplomatic partner in Asia plummeted from 63 per cent to 6 per cent.[8] South Koreans have also been concerned that the dynamism and growth of China's economy are pulling the North Korean economy, particularly in its northern provinces, into China's orbit and away from South Korea's. Many are also angered by China's forcible repatriation of North Korean refugees back to North Korea. In recent years, gaps have begun to open up between China's and South Korea's views of North Korea. As noted above, there was considerable anger over China's refusal to blame or sanction North Korea over the sinking of the *Cheonan* and the shelling of Yeonpyeong-do and, in the face of Pyongyang's increasing nuclear belligerence, there is growing annoyance at Beijing's opposition to South Korean deployment of anti-ballistic missile systems, particularly the Terminal High Altitude Area Defense (THAAD) ballistic missile defence system. More broadly, conservative South Koreans have been nonplussed at Beijing's unwillingness to discuss joint approaches to dealing with uncertainties regarding North Korea. Park herself expressed disappointment about the Xi government in China when Beijing did not return the hotline calls from the RoK President's office and the Ministry of National Defence immediately after the fourth nuclear test by Pyongyang. Such non-action by the Xi government indicated that Beijing's position toward the two Koreas had not changed in any fundamental ways and this was especially disappointing, even humiliating, to the Park administration, which made the controversial decision, despite its diplomatic and security ties with the 'West', to attend the celebration in Beijing in commemoration of the 70th anniversary of victory of the Chinese people over the Japanese and fascism.

The impact of the rise of China on the RoK–US alliance provides some important insights into the dynamics of the alliance. It shows how tightly focused South Korean security perceptions are on North Korea, as well

---

8   Terence Roehrig, 'History as a Strategic Weapon: The Korean and Chinese Struggle Over Koguryo', *Journal of Asian and African Studies*, vol. 45, no. 1, Feb. 2010, pp. 5–28. doi. org/10.1177/0021909610352675.

as how pragmatically South Korean calculations about their security and economic interest shift in relation to changing power dynamics in their region.[9] In recent years, as both Seoul and Beijing have begun to engage with Japan on trilateral economic cooperation, South Korea's existential but pragmatic interest in the evolving shape of North-East Asia has become manifest. Despite years of courtship of China and frustration with the United States, the bedrock of the alliance remains undisturbed, showing Seoul to be interested in simultaneously bandwagoning with a rising China, but not at the cost of its balancing alliance with the United States, while the strategic balance in North-East Asia evolves into a new status quo.

Alliance Asymmetries

By definition, every alliance with the world's sole superpower is an asymmetric relationship. And yet, a major source of tension in the RoK–US alliance has been the combination of *stable* and *evolving* asymmetries. In a situation of stable asymmetries, an alliance is able to develop mechanisms for their management or, in the case that they are not resolved or managed—such as the decades-old dispute between the United States and its NATO allies over military spending—they become progressively uncontroversial and effectively quarantined from disturbing the broader alliance. In an alliance with evolving asymmetries—for example, between the United States and the United Kingdom in light of London's changing capabilities in nuclear and conventional weapons—the alliance becomes a shock-absorbing mechanism, facilitating an integrated response to the changing capabilities of each partner. However, the combination of stability and evolution in the RoK–US alliance's asymmetries has been a very difficult combination for the alliance to manage.

The most pronounced stable asymmetry in the RoK–US alliance has been the sovereign status of each of the parties. South Korea's sovereignty has been truncated and compromised by the continued presence of US troops for more than six decades, and there is a strong sense in South Korea that the bedrock of the alliance lies in this continuing abnormality. This is only heightened by growing discussion of Japan's security 'normalisation' in both Tokyo and Washington, giving rise to an acute awareness in

9   Hyon Joo Yoo, 'The Korea–US Alliance as a Source of Creeping Tension: A Korean Perspective', *Asian Perspective*, vol. 36, no. 2, Apr.–Jun. 2012, pp. 331–51.

South Korea that Japan's sovereign abnormality is being resolved while the prospects of a similar resolution for South Korea are slight. In the context of this sensitivity to sovereignty in North-East Asia, the stability of the regional order is hostage to the 'tyranny of small issues', where disputes over islands, for example, are able to highjack progressive trust- and order-building. There is a counterpart 'tyranny of small voices' in which US allies are increasing their demands on their alliance partner, thereby hindering Washington's capacity to develop a coherent strategic vision for the region. In the absence of this vision, US policy appears increasingly Manichean—bent on classifying allies according to whether, in America's judgement, they are with the United States or with China (and by implication against the United States). Another stable asymmetry lies in the strategic outlook of the two parties: while South Korea's interests are regional and political-economic, those of the United States are global and political-military.[10]

The evolving asymmetries relate to the changing balance of material capabilities between the two allies. At the time of the signing of the Mutual Defence Treaty, the South Korean economy was 0.1 per cent the size of the American economy and, in per capita terms, South Koreans were just 10 per cent as wealthy as Americans. By 2015, the South Korean economy was 10 per cent the size of the American economy, and South Koreans were 70 per cent as wealthy as Americans on a per capita basis. No other US alliance has seen such a dramatic shift in the material asymmetry between two allies. The dramatic change in the material asymmetry of the alliance has had several implications. While the United States has been gratified by South Korea's success, and certainly prefers a stable, capable and wealthy ally, South Korea's rise has created expectations in Washington that it should play a more assertive role in regional security, particularly against what Washington believes is the challenge of a revanchist China to the stable order in the region. On the South Korean side, the success of its economy in high-technology innovation and production has created expectations that Seoul should no longer be the passive purchaser of advanced US military technology, but rather should increasingly invest in developing its own defence technologies. This tension has underpinned some of the delays and disagreements concerning the integration of South Korean and American missile defence deployments in the region. Another change on the South

---

10   Kang, 'Rising Powers, Offshore Balancers', 2005, p. 32.

Korean side has been democratisation and the emergence of a dynamic and influential civil society, greatly restricting the freedom of manoeuvre within the alliance that democratic South Korean governments can enjoy in comparison to their authoritarian predecessors.

The change in material asymmetry has led to a questioning within the South Korean security elite of just how closely the RoK's security interests align with those of the United States. An ally that has for decades gratefully accepted a place under the American nuclear extended-deterrence umbrella has begun to consider how it might look to its own resources to defend itself. A 2014 national survey by the Asan Institute for Policy Studies found that 52.8 per cent of respondents say that they believe the United States will intervene for South Korea in case of a war, that 54.4 per cent believe that North Korea will use nuclear weapons in case of another Korean War, and that 52.2 per cent believe that the United States will use its nuclear weapons if North Korea launches nuclear attacks on the South. Tellingly, 61.3 per cent of respondents agreed that South Korea needs to develop its own nuclear weapons.[11] Interestingly, the fewest respondents who believed South Korea should develop nuclear weapons thought it should do so to counter North Korea's nuclear threat (32.2 per cent), more advocated nuclear weapons in order to increase South Korea's international influence (33.5 per cent), and to possess nuclear sovereignty as an independent country (33.4 per cent).

This combination of stable and evolving asymmetries has led to a potent mixture in terms of managing the alliance relationship. The growing sense of South Korean capacity and national pride rubs up repeatedly against its sense of compromised sovereignty in ways that affect the alliance's dynamics. To date, the allies have managed these issues, but this is no guarantee for the future. Since 2009, the alliance has been upgraded from a specific undertaking against a North Korean attack to a regional and even a global partnership. Seoul has embarked on a new phase of middle-power activism, engaging enthusiastically in regional forums and global bodies, such as the G20, in ways that have enhanced rather than detracted from the alliance. The two sides are edging closer on ballistic missile defence, deciding on a policy of interoperability rather than integration. A process of relocation of US forces from the area of the Korean demilitarised zone to other parts of South Korea is progressing, and a new

11   *South Korean Attitudes Toward North Korea and Reunification*, Asan Institute Report, Feb. 2014.

cost-sharing arrangement for the financial support of US forces in Korea has been pragmatically negotiated. The only sticking point has been in the transition from the operational control of US and South Korean forces in wartime by a US commander; a 2007 agreement to split the United States Forces Korea Combined Forces Command into separate US and RoK commands has been delayed in the face of North Korea's aggression and concerns about the readiness of RoK forces for independent response to an attack. The postponement of the wartime operational control transfer without any set date for its enactment has created anxiety in South Korean society that the RoK military lacks resolve and a sense of responsibility for achieving self-defence.

Changing Role Conceptions

Of course, military alliances are not just about pragmatic security interests. A military alliance is a good barometer to measure the strength of mutual trust between countries based upon common values and world views. Forging a military alliance is not only determined by the purpose of deterring the projected military threat from a common adversary. A military alliance is also an institution that nations create to protect political ideology and key principles that they deem indispensable for maintaining civilised orders. For instance, as political scientist Tony Smith concludes in his book *America's Mission*, World War II marked the defeat—one immediate, and the other after four decades—of fascism and communism, the two totalitarian rivals of liberal democracy as viable forms of political organisation, not just a military victory by the allied powers.[12]

Enhancing a bilateral security partnership as a value-based military alliance is an ambitious goal for both sides. Under international anarchy, where there is no central authority above sovereign states to enforce promises between states, it might be regarded as a rarity that states tie their national security to pursuit of shared values. To realists, it is a futile and dangerous practice. Justifying your security alliance with values and principles is only useful as nice diplomatic rhetoric or a code word. And yet, in rhetoric if not always in action, this has been a distinguishing feature of US military alliances across the globe.

---

12 Tony Smith, *America's Mission: The United States and the Worldwide Struggle for Democracy*, Princeton University Press, 1995.

South Korea has a keen interest in this issue from the alliance perspective. Broadly speaking, it assesses the status of the RoK–US military alliance by two standards: functional and comparative. As for functional aspects, the South Korean Government and public assess the value of the alliance in terms of its contribution to national security, especially for maintaining sufficient and reliable deterrence and defence capability against military threats from North Korea. At the same time, South Koreans tend to use the US–Japan alliance as a measuring stick for US 'fairness' toward South Korea as its ally. The way the United States and Japan define the core missions and nature of their bilateral security alliance affects the way South Koreans expect the United States to define those of the RoK–US security alliance.

To many South Koreans, the RoK–US security partnership must be as qualified as the US–Japan security alliance is to become a global partnership based upon common values and historical views. Like Japan and the United States, South Korea and the United States have taken steady steps to elevate the status of their alliance to a value-based alliance. The 'Joint Vision for the Alliance of the United States of America and the Republic of Korea', which was announced on 16 June 2009, stipulated the commitment of both governments to 'build a comprehensive strategic alliance of bilateral, regional and global scope, based on common values and mutual trust'. The statement even tied the mission of the alliance to Korea's unification based upon shared values between the allies. It defines the purpose of the alliance as 'establishing a durable peace on the Peninsula and leading to peaceful reunification on the principles of free democracy and a market economy'. Such strategic vision is reiterated and articulated in the 2013 'Joint Declaration in Commemoration of the 60th Anniversary of the Alliance between the Republic of Korea and the United States of America', in which the two declared that the alliance:

> has evolved into a comprehensive strategic alliance with deep cooperation extending beyond security to also encompass the political, economic, cultural, and people-to-people realms. The freedom, friendship, and shared prosperity we enjoy today rest upon our shared values of liberty, democracy, and a market economy.

The 2013 declaration also affirmed that it is the basis of the joint vision that Korean unification should be achieved peacefully, and 'based upon the principles of denuclearization, democracy and a free market economy'.

Some may suggest that finding out whether the RoK–US alliance can be a genuine value-based security partnership in fulfilment of the official strategic visions is impossible until North Korea's military threat disappears. Only then will we be able to find out that the alliance was based upon mutual identity and common values, as in the case of NATO remaining robust even after the disappearance of the Soviet Union.

Conclusion

The RoK–US alliance presents some of the most confounding puzzles and practical dilemmas of any of America's alliances. It has confronted a constant and unpredictable threat for its entire existence and, more recently, is at the forefront of a rapidly shifting relative-power configuration in the Asia Pacific. It has embodied both stable and evolving asymmetries and a shift towards aspirations for a more values-based alliance partnership. And yet, through all of these challenges, the alliance has remained solid and relatively adaptable. Perhaps the key to thinking about the future of the alliance lies in the question of values. For a Manichean-minded United States, a values-based alliance will set natural limits on Seoul's willingness to bandwagon with a rising China. For a pragmatically minded South Korea, the evolution of the values question—probably involving Japan and yes, Taiwan also—will be key to the arrival of North-East Asia at a new stable status quo. For these reasons, perhaps we are right to view the RoK–US alliance as a bellwether for the evolution of other US alliances in this era of power transition.

5

Denmark's Fight Against Irrelevance, or the Alliance Politics of 'Punching Above Your Weight'

Kristian Søby Kristensen & Kristian Knus Larsen

At the official memorial service for Nelson Mandela on 13 December 2013, Roberto Schmidt, a photographer from Agence France-Presse (AFP), caught US President Barack Obama and UK Prime Minister David Cameron flanking Danish Prime Minister Helle Thorning-Schmidt while all three smiled and posed for a selfie. The picture immediately went viral and sparked global media debates ranging from how heads of state and government should behave at official events to whether Michelle Obama looked angry, jealous or just more interested in following the memorial service than in group selfies.[1]

In the context of Danish alliance politics, however, the symbolism of the picture carries more significant messages. In international relations, being positioned squarely and securely between the United States and the United Kingdom, and getting positive attention from both, to a large extent defines both the means and the ends of Danish security policy. Increasingly, and for the last decade or more, the core goals of Danish

---

1   As was the case, for instance, with UK newspaper the *Guardian* in which the selfie was 'portrayed as a mark of disrespect'. See Judith Soal, 'Barack Obama and David Cameron Pose for Selfie with Danish PM', *Guardian*, 11 Dec. 2013.

alliance politics have been to associate Denmark closely with and get the maximum amount of positive attention from the United States first and foremost.

This policy has, surprisingly to many, been consistent across governments and incurred tangible costs in both Danish blood and treasure while providing only more intangible Danish political gains. It has further positioned Denmark rather high on the US calling list as Denmark has shown itself to be a dependable and willing source of support for US military initiatives, as was the case, for instance, in the intervention in Libya in 2011. This policy concurrently sets Denmark apart from many other European small states, which have not to the same degree been willing or able to associate themselves so closely with the United States in international politics.

Andreas Løvold argues that, in today's international relations, small states—like Denmark—do not face threats to their survival. On the contrary, they face the threat of being left without influence, the threat of being irrelevant in international relations.[2] In many ways, Danish alliance politics seem to have taken Løvold's argument to heart. Consequently, Danish alliance politics can be seen as a continuous fight against irrelevance. In the Danish political version of this argument, that has meant constantly seeking closeness with the United States and status as a relevant actor. It has also meant being a country that, in the eyes of American decision-makers, 'punches above its weight' in international affairs.[3]

While not only setting Denmark apart from many other European small states, this unambiguously close relationship and almost unconditional support for US international policies marks also a historical departure from a radically different historical past, where Danish foreign policy was, if not in direct opposition to, then at least hesitant in its support of American policies and ambiguous in regards to the Danish political commitment to NATO and the transatlantic system of alliance. Consequently, this chapter does three things. First, this fundamental historical change is unpacked. That leads, secondly, to a characterisation of the relation

---

2   Andreas Løvold, 'Småstatsproblematikken i Internasjonal Politkk', *Internajsonal Politikk*, vol. 62, no. 1, 2004, pp. 7–31.
3   'Remarks by President Obama, Danish Prime Minister Rasmussen', IIP Digital, United States of America Embassy, 14 Mar. 2011, viewed Aug. 2016, www.gpo.gov/fdsys/pkg/DCPD-201100173/pdf/DCPD-201100173.pdf.

between a current militarised Danish foreign policy and core assumptions of Danish alliance politics. Third, the chapter explains this radical and seemingly continuous change of politics through the convergence of different political rationales in Danish alliance politics, in Danish–US relations and in the view of the US role in the world. In conclusion, the paper argues that this shift in politics is, on the one hand, relatively solid and is increasingly being taken for granted. On the other hand, however, the chapter identifies a number of challenges that may contribute to change in Danish alliance politics.

Danish Alliance Politics: A Brief History

With the end of the Cold War, Denmark's geopolitical position changed radically. Instead of being a frontline state in a global confrontation, Denmark could see, not the end of history, but world history move away from Denmark. This is equally reflected in subsequent Danish defence and security white papers noting a continuously more secure regional environment, culminating in a 2008 white paper that was unable to identify any territorial threat to Denmark in the foreseeable future and characterised the Danish security environment as benign 'without historical precedent'.[4]

Danish politicians were not slow to recognise that this fundamental change in European geopolitics would also change both the conditions and the opportunities for Danish foreign and security policy. Danish foreign policy had been perceived as reactive and pragmatic during the last decades of the Cold War, and the end of the Cold War meant that a new line of policy was both possible and necessary. Supported by the Ministry of Foreign Affairs, the conservative–liberal government formulated a more active and value-based Danish foreign policy. From the beginning, this policy focused on positioning Denmark as actively contributing to building and maintaining international institutional architecture in Europe, thereby ensuring simultaneously the new pan-European peace, anchoring a reunited Germany institutionally in what was then the European Economic Community and, through NATO, keeping the United States as the ultimate underwriter of European

---

4   Danish Government, *Dansk Forsvar, Globalt Engagement: Beretning fra Forsvarskommissionen af 2008*, Ministry of Defence, 2009, p. 36, viewed Aug. 2016, www.fmn.dk/videnom/Documents/Hovedbind-FKOM-2008-beretning.pdf.

security.[5] In 1993 the conservative-liberal government was replaced by a social democratic government. This entailed few changes in the line of policy re-emphasising the importance of liberal ideas and multilateral institutions.[6] But, simultaneously, this more active policy acquired a military dimension as Denmark, for the first time since World War II, deployed military force in the form of a navy ship in support of the US-led coalition in the Gulf War of 1991.

While only symbolic in nature and far away from any combat operations, the decision to employ Danish military assets marked a fundamental shift in Danish decision-makers' view on the role of Danish military force in foreign policy and alliance politics. Whereas a US request for Danish military assistance in 1952 for the war effort in Korea was met with the counteroffer of a hospital ship, in the Gulf War and in post–Cold War geopolitics, it seems legitimate in the milieu of the new activist Danish foreign policy to use military force—far away from Danish territory and to maintain international order. Subsequently, the Danish armed forces engaged in the peacekeeping missions of the 1990s in an attempt to end the bloodshed of the Balkan Wars. Denmark's engagements in the former Yugoslavia showed a country that was prepared to participate in potentially dangerous peacekeeping operations and Danish participation in the Kosovo campaign in 1999 showed that a UN Security Council authorisation was not a precondition for Danish use of force. Instead, NATO was increasingly seen as the most important international institution and American leadership as the most important factor for peace and security in Europe.

When NATO invoked Article 5 the day after the 9/11 terrorist attacks in the United States in 2001, it was a decision wholeheartedly supported by Denmark. Danish politicians expected that a military response would be organised through the UN or NATO.[7] Instead, the United States opted for a more unilateral response in Afghanistan in 2001–02 and, even more contentiously, in 2003 in the Iraq War. The liberal-conservative Danish Government that took office in November 2001 unequivocally followed its American allies into war. Denmark's choice between Europe and the

5   Rasmus Brus Pedersen, 'Danish Foreign Policy Activism: Differences in Kind or Degree', *Cooperation and Conflict*, vol. 47, no. 3, 2012, pp. 331–49. doi.org/10.1177/0010836712444863.
6   Rasmus Brus Pedersen, 'Fra Aktiv Internationalisme til International Aktivisme: Udvikling og Tendenser i Dansk Udenrigspolitisk Aktivisme', *Politica*, vol. 44, no. 1, 2012, pp. 111–30.
7   Pedersen, 'Fra Aktiv Internationalisme til International Aktivisme', 2012.

United States, or the United States and the United Nations, often falls with the United States, leading Hans Mouritzen to coin Danish alliance politics as 'super atlanticist'.[8]

Denmark has been a persistent ally to the United States throughout the wars in Afghanistan and Iraq and unquestionably supported US policies in both countries as well as in the wider Middle East. Instead of being a reluctant ally, Denmark has worked hard to become and remain an 'impeccable'[9] US ally. This has established Denmark as a core NATO member, a dependable US diplomatic ally and a consistent contributor to US-led military coalitions. This consistent political support, combined with a willingness to stay the course, take risks and participate with no official caveats in military operations has not gone unnoticed in Washington. Peter Viggo Jakobsen recounts a British delegation to Washington in 2013 being told by a top official of the Obama administration that the United Kingdom ought to be more like Denmark, 'a model to follow'.[10] If Danish alliance politics are about fighting for relevance and attention from the United States, then being set up as a model for the United Kingdom is indeed a mark of success.

The development of this increasingly close alliance relationship between Denmark and the United States is to a wide extent based on a specific Danish view on the use of armed force that sets Denmark apart from many comparable European small states. The continuously closer US–Danish relationship goes hand in hand with the militarisation of Danish foreign policy, where use of Danish armed force has become an increasingly legitimate and pivotal foreign and alliance policy tool.

The Militarisation of Danish Foreign Policy

On 29 April 1994, Serbian forces ambushed a squadron of Danish Leopard 1 main battle tanks that was in Bosnia as part of UN Protection Force (UNPROFOR). In the firefight taking place over the next two hours, the Danish forces manage to destroy the Serbian attackers and return to

8   Hans Mouritzen, 'Denmark's Super Atlanticism', *Journal of Transatlantic Studies*, vol. 5, no. 2, 2007, pp. 155–67. doi.org/10.1080/14794019908656861.
9   Jens Ringsmose & Sten Rynning, 'The Impeccable Ally? Denmark, NATO and the Uncertain Future of Top-Tier Membership', in Nanna Hvidt & Hans Mouritzen (eds), *Danish Foreign Policy Yearbook 2008*, Copenhagen: Danish Institute for International Studies, 2008, pp. 55–84.
10   Peter Viggo Jakobsen & Jens Ringsmose, 'Size and Reputation – Why the USA Has Valued its "Special Relationship" with Denmark and the UK differently since 9/11', *Journal of Transatlantic Studies*, vol. 13. no. 2, pp. 135–53.

base without casualties, thus proving possible a more muscular approach to peacekeeping.[11] Later, Michael Rose, UNPROFOR commander, stated that 'the Danish tanks changed the way to solve wider peacekeeping tasks forever'.[12] They did more than that, however. They equally changed the view on the use of force by Danish foreign policy elites, making 'peace operations … the flagship in the new activist foreign policy pursued by Denmark in the 1990s'.[13]

Successive Danish governments have used the term activism to describe a basic component of their foreign policy, denoting a more (supposedly more than before) active Danish profile in the international sphere and that Denmark would pursue its values and interests actively around the world. Both centre-right (liberal-conservative) and centre-left (social democratic) governments have increasingly used the Danish armed forces as a key component or tool of this active foreign policy. This use of armed force abroad as a central instrument of Danish foreign policy makes it possible even to label Danish foreign policy as military activism.[14]

Jakobsen defines military activism as the use of armed force in international engagements for purposes that exceed Denmark's narrow national defence.[15] Thus, military activism is more than self-defence. It is about the use of armed force to influence international developments, but it is also about increasing Danish status and visibility among key Danish partners and allies. In a comparative perspective, and dating back to the tank engagement in Bosnia, Denmark has been unusually willing to deploy military force. Denmark's so-called military activism has led Danish decision-makers to adopt a remarkable risk-prone profile. Risk-taking and few national restrictions (caveats) have been notable features of Denmark's military activism.[16] Consequently, the Danish Government supported the US invasion of Iraq in 2003, and a comfortable parliamentary majority decided to deploy Danish land forces to help stabilise Iraq after combat

11   Ole Kjeld Hansen, 'Operation "Bøllebank"', *Dansk Militaerhistorie*, 28 Oct. 2013, viewed Aug. 2016, milhist.dk/slaget/operation-bollebank/.
12   Quoted in Peter Viggo Jakobsen, *Nordic Approaches to Peace Operations: A New Model in the Making*, London & New York: Routledge, 2006, p. 83.
13   Jakobsen, *Nordic Approaches to Peace Operations*, 2006, p. 109.
14   Kristian Søby Kristensen, *Danmark i Krig: Demokrati, Politik og Strategi i den Militære Aktivisme*, Copenhagen: DJØF Forlag, 2013.
15   Peter Viggo Jakobsen, 'Danmarks Militære Aktivisme Fortsætter Med Eller Uden USA', *Politik*, vol. 18, no. 4, 2015, pp. 5–13.
16   Karsten Jakob Møller & Peter Viggo Jakobsen, 'Good News: Libya and the Danish Way of War', in Nanna Hvidt & Hans Mouritzen (eds), *Danish Foreign Policy Yearbook 2012*, Copenhagen: Danish Institute for International Studies, 2012, pp. 106–30.

operations were deemed to be over. Working with the British in Basra region, the Danish forces quickly found themselves engaged in what ended up being the losing side of a counterinsurgency operation costing eight Danish lives.

It is, however, the 2006 decision to deploy—again with the British—to the Helmand Province in Afghanistan that symbolically, and in terms of both human and economic costs, stands out as the most significant example of Danish military activism. In Helmand's 'green zone' a Danish battalion battle group conducted frequent and intense combat operations fighting the Taliban, and the number of casualties increased dramatically, especially in the years 2007–11.

That the operation could lead to heavy fighting was not lost on the Danish Defence Command. In addition to the risks associated with the deployment to Helmand, however, the top echelon of the Danish armed forces equally saw this as, first, an opportunity to provide a distinct Danish military contribution to the development of Helmand. Second, to show Danish politicians that their armed forces could function in a militarily activist foreign policy. And third, by combining both of the above, prove their own 'military metier', as stated by then Chief of Defence General Hans Jesper Helsø.[17] Consequently, both the Danish armed forces and Danish political decision-makers went to Helmand with their eyes relatively open, knowing the risk involved. In Afghanistan, by 2013 the Danish forces had suffered 43 casualties and more than 200 seriously wounded,[18] making Denmark the country with the highest number of fatalities relative to the size of its population of all those contributing troops to the International Security Assistance Force (ISAF).

The government's decision to deploy troops to Helmand was supported by a broad majority of the Danish parliament and, perhaps surprising to the government itself and despite rising casualties, public support remained relatively constant with between 40–50 per cent of Danes supporting the mission. This leaves Denmark changing places with the United States as the two ISAF countries with the highest public support for the operations in Afghanistan (between 2006 and 2011).[19]

---

17   Quoted in Mikkel Vedby Rasmussen, *Den Gode Krig*, Copenhagen: Gyldendal, 2011.
18   'Combat Mission in Afghanistan is over', *CPH Post Online*, 22 Jul. 2013.
19   Peter Viggo Jakobsen & Jens Ringsmose, 'In Denmark, Afghanistan is Worth Dying for: How Public Support for the War was Maintained in the Face of Mounting Casualties and Elusive Success', *Cooperation and Conflict*, vol. 50, no. 2, 2014, pp. 211–27. doi.org/10.1177/0010836714545688.

Looking at the apparent appetite for warfare that had developed in Denmark, it should come as no surprise that the Danish Government did not hesitate to offer a Danish military contribution when NATO started preparing Operation Unified Protector as a response to the conflict in Libya. Indeed, the then Minister of Foreign Affairs called it 'good news' when the government had gotten parliamentary backing to deploy Danish F-16s to the effort against Libyan leader Muammar Gaddafi's forces.[20]

All parties in parliament, including the radical socialist left wing, supported the decision and no critical questions were asked by the media when the Minister of Foreign Affairs announced the deployment. Six F-16s took off for Sicily at such a pace that only French, American and British aircrafts were in place before them.[21] Denmark put no national restrictions on the use of its aircraft. The Danish F-16s took a central role in the operations and the Joint Force Air Component Commander, Major-General Margaret H Woodward, of the US Operation Odyssey Dawn called the Danish F-16s the 'rock stars of the campaign' due to their versatility.[22] The flexible character of the Danish contribution was supplemented with a large amount of precision-guided munitions. According to the RAND Corporation, '[the Norwegian and Danish] air forces proved critical to maintain pressure on Muammar Qaddafi's regime'.[23] Thus, RAND concludes that the Danish air force 'made a contribution to Libya operations out of proportion to its size, both quantitatively and qualitatively'.[24] Equally, when US Secretary of Defense Robert Gates in 2011 lambasted European allies in general for their lack of political will and military capability, the efforts of the Danish air force in Libya was noted as a positive exception to both things lacking in wider Europe. Libya thus becomes a perfect example of the use of force in Danish alliance politics. It positions Denmark as a relevant and noticed ally, contributing more than expected.

In sum, when looking at the above examples of Danish use of force under the foreign policy heading of military activism, a number of characteristics are worth noting. First, political as well as military risk-taking have been prevalent and, in comparative perspective, a significant feature of Danish

---

20   Annelise Hartmann Eskesen, 'Lene Espersen: Jeg Har to Gode Nyheder', *Politiken*, 18 Mar. 2011.

21   Møller & Jakobsen, 'Good News', 2012.

22   Møller & Jakobsen, 'Good News', 2012.

23   Karl P Mueller, *Precision and Purpose: Airpower in the Libyan Civil War*, Washington DC: Rand Corporation, 2015.

24   Mueller, *Precision and Purpose*, 2015.

use of military force. By agreeing to operate in dangerous or difficult areas without many national restrictions or caveats, Danish politicians have accepted an increased risk of casualties. But more risks follow. Danish politicians have additionally accepted the political risks of potentially causing civilian casualties, of taking political responsibility for potentially unpopular—and sometimes unwinnable—military operations and, finally, accepted the political risk incurred by delegating control of Danish armed forces, without caveats, to allied or coalition command.

Second, the colour of government has had limited influence on Danish use of force, and both centre-right and centre-left governments have enjoyed wide parliamentary support as well as positive public opinion in response to their decisions to use force abroad. This has meant that shifting governments have been able not only to use force abroad, but to prioritise the speed of the decision-making process with which Denmark decides to use military force—as was the case in Libya. This in itself is an indication of the degree to which military activism and the use of force has become a constant feature of Danish foreign policy, setting Denmark apart as a special case compared to other Nordic or European countries.[25] The active use of force has been a consistent feature of Danish foreign policy, the continuity of which has surprised many engaged with the analysis of Danish foreign policy.[26]

In the following we ask why this is so, and why this feature has been so consistent and prevalent. Our answer is that the special Danish willingness to use force needs to be understood as a specific conflation of three distinct political rationalities guiding Danish foreign policy. This has, in turn, made possible the ever closer alliance with the United States. Denmark has—because of this conflation—been able to maintain the political and public support required to incur the costs necessary to constantly be relevant to and noticed by American decision-makers. Just as Gates noted, the Danish contribution to the Libya campaign showed Denmark to be punching above its weight.

25   See Hakon Lunde Saxi, 'Defending Small States: Norwegian and Danish Defense Policies in the Post-Cold War Era', *Defense and Security Analysis*, vol. 26, no. 4, 2010, pp. 415–30. doi.org/10.1080/14751798.2010.534649.
26   See Ringsmose & Rynning, 'The Impeccable Ally?', 2008, pp. 55–84.

Why? Convergence of Three Rationales in Danish Alliance Politics

On 26 September 2014, then Danish Prime Minister Helle Thorning-Schmidt announced that Denmark would contribute F-16s in the fight against Islamic State. At the press conference, the Prime Minister reminded the journalists present that 'Denmark is one of those countries that have already taken responsibility', and then informed them that 'Denmark last night received a formal request from the US … for, among others, Danish F-16s'.[27] The Prime Minister had already in the morning informally contacted key parliament leaders to make sure the deployment could be voted through parliament the following week. The first question from the press addressed not the risks, mission parameters or the strategy of the operation, but the pace of the decision-making process: 'You hope that it will be possible to summon the Parliament and pass the bill already next week. What will that mean in terms of getting the planes in the air?' The Prime Minister replied that 'the planes can be in the air as soon as the bill is passed by Parliament. Luckily, we can deliver quickly.'[28]

The bill was passed by approximately 90 per cent of the votes in the parliament, and the F-16s took off a week after the request was received. In the public debate about use of force, the question is not if, but how fast. The almost automatic reaction to the American request was not surprising, however. A year before, the Prime Minister participated in a dinner hosted by Fredrik Reinfeldt—then Swedish Prime Minister—on the occasion of President Obama visiting Sweden. Also present were the heads of state and government of Finland, Iceland and Norway. Prior to the meeting, Sweden, Norway and Finland had refused to participate in any intervention punishing the Syrian regime for its use of chemical weapons against its own civilian population. Denmark, on the other hand, had announced that it, without any indications of US intentions or plans, would support the United States against the regime of Bashar al-Assad. Thorning-Schmidt emphasised that it was important to 'signal to the Americans that they have a very close ally here that they can count on'.[29]

---

27   Helle Thorning-Schmidt, 'Prime Minister's Press Conference September 26 2014', Statsministeriet, viewed Aug. 2016, www.stm.dk/_p_14084.html.

28   Thorning-Schmidt, 'Prime Minister's Press Conference September 26 2014'.

29   Helle Thorning-Schmidt, 'Thorning Lover Støtte til Obama', *TV 2 Nyhederne*, 3 Sep. 2013, viewed Aug. 2016, nyhederne.tv2.dk/article.php/id-71152061:thorning-lover-obama-st%C3%B8tte-i-syrien.html.

The unequivocal support for any potential US military action against Assad, as well as the pace of the decision-making process and the political unity in the parliament in the case of a US request for military support against ISIS show how established the use of force has become in Danish foreign policy and how this is linked to Denmark's special relationship with the United States.

Traditional foreign policy analysis would emphasise that these decisions are based on a calculation of Danish interests and values in relation to a particular political interpretation of the international environment. Møller and Jakobsen thus identify three primary objectives: to protect Danish territorial integrity, promote and protect Danish values and to 'do our part' as a trustworthy partner.[30] While all these objectives are significant, it is difficult to see how these objectives should set Denmark radically apart from its Nordic neighbours, following often very different policies. Similarly, explaining Denmark's particular military activism on particular domestic policies of shifting governing parties, on the other hand, fails to explain the significant continuity across governments.[31]

To make sense of this almost instinctive and unconditional military and political support to American military operations as well as the continued willingness by large parts of the Danish public and political establishment to take risks and use military force, we argue that three long-standing rationalities in Danish foreign policy converge, reinforcing simultaneously the use of force and the US–Danish relationship. Building on Mikkel Vedby Rasmussen—who debates Danish strategic culture as a reflection of changes in the relation between two discourses on the utility of force in international relations[32]—we show the value of analysing Danish alliance politics, as being a consequence of long-term historical convergences of a cosmopolitan, a strategic and a moral rationale for Danish use of force.

The cosmopolitan rationale is based on the idea that Western use of force can be a universal force for good. The air campaign against Serbia in the spring of 1999 was aimed at stopping human rights violations occurring in Kosovo. The bill that was presented to the Danish parliament read: 'Folketinget [the Danish Parliament] hereby declares its consent to send

---

30   Møller & Jakobsen, 'Good News', 2012.
31   See Pedersen, 'Danish Foreign Policy Activism', 2012, pp. 331–49.
32   Mikkel Vedby Rasmussen, '"What's the Use of It?": Danish Strategic Culture and the Utility of Armed Force', *Cooperation and Conflict*, vol. 40, no. 1, 2005, pp. 67–89. doi. org/10.1177/0010836705049735.

a Danish contribution to the NATO efforts in the Western Balkans to prevent a humanitarian catastrophe in Kosovo'.[33] As the air campaign unfolded in April 1999, Danish Defence Minister Hans Hækkerup expressed the cosmopolitan view: 'Kosovo can become the example of how it is necessary to go in and apply the necessary pressure to solve things out … NATO will not draw any geographical boundaries describing where the Alliance can act'.[34] The engagement in Kosovo showed how military force could safeguard human rights. The words of Hækkerup, who describes NATO acting without boundaries, today seems like a succinct prophecy for the following decade. The cosmopolitan rationale was upheld through the 2000s, as humanitarian concerns have been central to political arguments for why Denmark deployed or maintained a military presence in, for instance, Kosovo, Iraq, Afghanistan or Mali.

Cosmopolitan concerns were thus repeatedly emphasised during the Danish engagement in Afghanistan. While 9/11 and the terrorist threat were accentuated, so was the need to focus on humanitarian development. In 2008, Danish Minister of Foreign Affairs Per Stig Møller and Minister for International Development Ulla Tørnæs explained Denmark's strategy in Afghanistan:

> The goal is to stabilise Afghanistan, to ensure that the democratic elected government is the only master of the house and to ensure higher standards of living, human rights and democracy for the Afghan population … Human rights are now ensured in the constitution, and a human rights commission has been established with Danish support.[35]

Parallel arguments can be found in relation to more recent deployments of Danish armed forces. In Denmark the intervention in Libya was seen as the international community coming together acting to prevent genocide. Thus it made sense for conservative Minister of Foreign Affairs Lene Espersen, as noted above, to declare it a 'good thing' that Danish military action was forthcoming. Equally, in deciding to deploy F-16s to fight ISIS

---

33   Danish Parliament, 'Forslag til Folketingsbeslutning om et Dansk Militært Bidrag til en NATO-Indsats på det Vestlige Balkan', Motion no. B4, Copenhagen, 1998.

34   Morten Jastrup, 'NATO er Uden Begrænsninger', *Information*, 21 Apr. 1999, viewed Aug. 2016, www.information.dk/29859.

35   P S Møller & U Tørnæs, 'Derfor er vi i Afghanistan', *Politiken*, 16 Jan. 2008, viewed Aug. 2016, politiken.dk/debat/kroniken/ECE458081/derfor-er-vi-i-afghanistan/.

in Iraq, the bill authorising Danish use of force repeatedly emphasises humanitarian concerns, human rights violations and an international responsibility to help Iraqi authorities protect its civilian population.[36]

The strategic rationale, also associated with the use of force, is in Danish alliance politics about being closely aligned with the United States and providing political and military support when requested by the US Government. Thorning-Schmidt was open about this in 2013 when she declared that Denmark would support American actions in Syria even before the US Government had declared that it would take action, and what that action would entail. As British support foundered in the House of Commons, Denmark found itself—together with France—as the only European country openly supporting American-led military action in Syria. This made Denmark stand out in Europe, in what seemed like a peculiar position for a Scandinavian small state. But, if the strategic goal is closeness, attention and relevance vis-à-vis the United States, it is an almost perfect position.

This reflects the strategic rationale in Danish politics. Maintaining a close relationship with the United States is not a new element in Danish alliance politics—indeed, this rationale was emphasised throughout the 2000s. With liberal Anders Fogh Rasmussen as Prime Minister, building ties with the United States was a core concern and, consequently, Denmark developed a close bilateral—and personal—relationship with the administration of George W Bush in the years after 9/11.

In September 2003, Rasmussen established the main lines in his government's alliance politics, and why that, for instance, entailed Danish support for the American invasion of Iraq:

> We are in the middle of a showdown with the policy of adaptation, which has dominated Danish foreign policy since the defeat [to Prussia] in 1864 … Cooperation with the US is not adaptation. It is equal cooperation with a friend, a partner, an ally, who honour the same principles and values as we do: democracy, freedom of speech, market economy, and human rights.[37]

---

36 Danish Parliament, 'Proposal for a Parliamentary Resolution for Additional Danish Military Contribution to Support the Fight Against ISIL', Motion no. B123, Copenhagen, 30 Sep. 2014, viewed Aug. 2016, www.ft.dk/samling/20131/beslutningsforslag/b123/bilag/1/1403349.pdf.
37 Anders Fogh Rasmussen, 'Statsminister Anders Fogh Rasmussens tale på Københavns Universitet den, 23 September 2003, "Visioner om Danmarks aktive Europapolitik"', viewed Aug. 2016, www.stm.dk/_p_7451.html.

In order to safeguard these principles and values, close cooperation with the United States is, for Rasmussen, self-evident. Per Stig Møller, as Minister of Foreign Affairs in Rasmussen's government, later elaborated: 'The USA is incredibly important to us. If we find ourselves in a crisis it will be the US that can help us. No one else can help us.'[38] The quid pro quo of this strategic calculation is that if Denmark needs to be able to count on the United States in a crisis, the best way to ensure that is to make sure the United States can count on Denmark. Rasmussen's liberal-conservative government continuously emphasised this strategic rationale through the 2000s and so did Thorning-Schmidt's social-democratic government, as shown above.

While Møller emphasises that the strategically motivated partnership with the United States is about a reinforced security guarantee, it is also about privileged access and influence. As stated by Rasmussen:

> At present I will say that Denmark has a unique strong position in international and European politics. Internationally we have direct access to the top political leadership in the US, the world's only superpower, and the only state that has global reach. Of course that does not mean that we can control such a state's foreign and security policy … But all things being equal, it makes Denmark a more interesting partner for negotiations and conversations.[39]

During his time in office, Rasmussen visited President Bush seven times, and Danish diplomats enjoyed increased access to Washington. Thorning-Schmidt's selfie with Cameron and Obama symbolises the strategic rationale of close alignment with the United States.

Lastly, Danish alliance politics has been formed by a moral rationale that rests on a distinct moral historiographic understanding of Danish foreign and alliance politics during World War II and the Cold War, making it, as noted by Karsten Møller and Jakobsen, morally necessary for Danish decision-makers today to 'do our part'. In his book on Denmark's war effort in Afghanistan, Mikkel Vedby Rasmussen highlights that one of the core principles of Danish military activism has been that Denmark should fight shoulder to shoulder with the United States and the United Kingdom

---

38   PS Møller, 'Danmark skal være en allieret, som USA altid kan regne med', *Information*, 20 Jul. 2015, viewed Aug. 2016, www.information.dk/539896.
39   Anders Fogh Rasmussen, quoted in A Henriksen & J Ringsmose, 'Hvad fik Danmark ud af det? Iraq, Afghanistan og forholdet til Washington', DIIS Rapport 2011:14, Copenhagen: Danish Institute for International Studies, 2011, p. 8.

because that is the right thing to do.[40] The importance of this principle was highlighted by Anders Fogh Rasmussen in repeated statements in the early 2000s. At the brink of the Iraqi invasion in March 2003 the Prime Minister thus argued that 'world history is filled with such dilemmas [of going to war]. And we would not be where we are today, if we or others had chosen to do nothing. There are situations where it is necessary to choose the uncomfortable option to ensure freedom and peace'.[41] In other words, had it not been for the United States and United Kingdom fighting in World War II, Denmark would not have been liberated from German occupation. Consequently, to pay that historical debt, Denmark cannot now do nothing, but is morally obligated to actively choose to do something.

In August 2003, Anders Fogh Rasmussen's government continued this line of reasoning and launched an attack on the Danish cooperative policy during most of the German occupation between 1940 and 1945. The Prime Minister stated: 'It has been of vital importance to Denmark's international reputation that we had a showdown with the policy of cooperation [during the German occupation]. Also for the way we see ourselves.'[42] In an op-ed, the Prime Minister further emphasised: 'Even judged on the premises of that time the Danish policy was naïve, and it is highly objectionable that the Danish political elite so strongly followed a policy of not only neutrality but active adaptation.'[43] In this way, current military activist policy is put forth as the morally right thing to do, as opposed to previous small state adaptation.

Denmark's historical debt was, according to Anders Fogh Rasmussen, now due, and Denmark's hesitant membership of the NATO alliance during the last decades of the Cold War further reinforced the need for Denmark to start down payments on its moral debt. That underlines the importance of the transatlantic alliance and entails supporting US policies, making hard but active choices, and bearing the costs and risks associated with using military force abroad. It is the right thing to do.

---

40   Mikkel Vedby Rasmussen, 'Den gode krig', *Gyldendal*, Copenhagen, 2011.
41   'Anders Fogh Rasmussens Tale Vedrørende Irak', 18 Mar. 2003, viewed Aug. 2016, danmarkshistorien.dk/leksikon-og-kilder/vis/materiale/anders-foghs-tale-vedroerende-irak-180303/?no_cache=1.
42   Anders Fogh Rasmussen, 'Opgøret med samarbejdspolitikken', Statsministeriet, 26 Aug. 2003, viewed Aug. 2016, www.stm.dk/_p_6393.html.
43   Anders Fogh Rasmussen, 'Fogh angriber samarbejdspolitikken', *DR Nyheder*, 29 Aug. 2003, viewed Aug. 2016, www.dr.dk/nyheder/htm/baggrund/tema2003/60%20aaret%20for%20bruddet/22.htm.

Taken together, these three rationales emphasise different reasons and objectives for the active use of military force and the significance of the transatlantic alliance. Combined with early lessons learned in the Balkans in the 1990s, they converge through a variety of arguments that have enabled broad political consensus in the Danish parliament and substantial and sustained public support for the use of force. Military deployments and political decisions have been mandated on the basis of bills and political debates that have drawn upon all three. Thus, the deployments to Afghanistan, Iraq, Libya, Mali and Iraq (again) were all founded on combinations of these rationales. Further, the military activist policy that is thus made possible and rational has enabled changing Danish governments to develop and maintain a position as a key NATO member and a close and dependable US ally. 'Punching above one's weight' to seek close relations with the United States makes sense from cosmopolitan, strategic and moral grounds. The United States is often the precondition for Danish force being a cosmopolitan force for good. Supporting US military actions is sound strategic realpolitik for a small state like Denmark. Finally, penance for past Danish foreign policy sins can be paid by standing by the United States.

Conclusions and Consequences

In July 2015, Danish servicemen warned against continued air operations in Iraq. Ground crews were exhausted and aircraft were increasingly in need of maintenance. The shop stewards in the Royal Danish Air Force, unusually and very publicly, asked Danish politicians 'to step up to their responsibility and withdraw the Danish contribution so the planes and mechanics can get a break'.[44] The aircraft returned to Denmark on 1 October only to see the Minister of Foreign Affairs, Kristian Jensen, responding to the November 2015 Paris terrorist attack by suggesting a redeployment of F-16s to Iraq.[45] The use of military force has become not only a key component in Danish foreign policy but also an accustomed practice.

---

44   H Jensen & JA Bjørnager, 'F-16 Mekanikere: Stop fly-aktionen mod Islamisk Stat', *Berlingske Tidenden*, 27 Jul. 2015, viewed Aug. 2016, www.b.dk/nationalt/f16-mekanikere-stop-fly-aktionen-mod-islamisk-stat.

45   Søren Ploug Lilmoes, 'Kristian Jensen: Regeringen er Klar til at Bombe i Syrien', *Politiko*, 15 Nov. 2015, viewed Aug. 2016, www.politiko.dk/nyheder/kristian-jensen-regeringen-er-klar-til-at-bombe-i-syrien.

The convergence of the cosmopolitan, the strategic and the moral rationale has entailed a sedimentation of the active use and political utility of military force in Danish alliance politics. Military force is what Denmark contributes within alliance settings and, due to consistent high public and broad political support for both NATO membership and participation in international military operations, the Danish politicians are not challenged to explain why military force is the right contribution. Instead of being just a label that describes current Danish alliance politics, military activism has become a foreign policy custom. The Danish public and politicians have become accustomed to sending Danish military forces to armed conflicts and, even though casualties have resulted in political discussions, it has not deterred the Danish parliament from repeatedly deploying military forces. Consequently, the current view on the use of force as a key component of Danish alliance-politics structure and lock-in-place Danish politics. Continuity is easy, whereas a new political course of action inevitably ends up in a difficult confrontation with some combination of the three rationales mentioned above.

Still, what may account for change if it is unlikely that an internally and politically driven break takes place? We highlight two potential sources of change. First, the current and future force structure of the Danish armed forces may increasingly be a deciding factor for how force can be used in Danish alliance politics. Second, perhaps military activism is not suited to the alliance politics of the future. The challenges that arose in Iraq with regard to the flight mechanics and aircraft can be seen in other areas of the Danish armed forces. A considerable number of capabilities are worn down, limited in numbers and need to be recapitalised. Thus, Denmark can still deploy fighter jets, tactical air lift, navy vessels, special operations forces and a battalion-sized task force, but the force structure is challenged in terms of sustainability.

Denmark has in the last decades—along with most Western European states—consistently spent less on defence and is currently spending 1.17 per cent of GDP, substantially off NATO's 2 per cent target. During the war in Afghanistan, Danish politicians and diplomats could argue that Denmark made a considerable contribution to the alliance through risk-taking. This has given rise to a notable discussion on whether member states should be assessed based on input, output or outcome measures. In other words, should alliance status be assessed on defence spending, deployable forces and capabilities, or *deployed* forces and capabilities? By always being willing to heed the call, and deploy forces, military activism has enabled Denmark to provide an outsized NATO contribution while keeping defence spending low. The cost has not been financial but increased risk to service personnel and a narrowing down of Danish capabilities.

With Russia's annexation of Crimea and its involvement in Eastern Ukraine, NATO's debate about defence spending has been re-emphasised, lessening the value of Danish risk-taking. So while Denmark's military activism proved a politically beneficial alliance policy in a world formed by the American 'war against terrorism' and subsequent counterinsurgency operations, it seems less likely to thrive in a world that is returning to geopolitics, with NATO increasingly focused on Russia, and the United States increasingly focused on China.

Military activism has—for a while—produced an equilibrium in Danish politics due to its ability to encompass cosmopolitan, strategic and moral rationales in Danish foreign policy, and simultaneously strengthening relations to the United States. Due to both internal and external factors, however, this could be changing. Denmark will in the coming years be challenged in balancing global, regional and Arctic demands. Denmark will need to refocus on the Nordic region and further develop policies and capabilities for the Arctic. Simultaneously, Denmark will be asked to contribute to collective defence in NATO. Doing that, while still being both able and willing to deploy military force out of area will be difficult for the very slim and not well-funded Danish force structure. Defence policy, for Denmark, immediately transforms into foreign and alliance politics.

In sum, military activism turned out to be a solid basis for consistent Danish alliance politics. The days of military activism might, however, be coming to an end. Not because of a critical and causality intolerant public or a war-weary parliament, but because of the slimming Danish force structure and because the key Danish ally—the United States—is now increasingly asking for defence spending rather than risk-taking.

6

Crusaders and Pragmatists: Australia Debates the American Alliance

Brendan Taylor & William T Tow

The most evident management challenge facing the US–Australia alliance going forward is how Canberra positions itself between its leading trading partner (a rising China) and its long-standing strategic ally (the United States). For more than half a decade now—ever since the former senior defence official turned professor Hugh White sparked a public discussion on the subject—this has been the dominant foreign policy debate in Australia. It is a debate that has attracted international attention including, most significantly, in Washington.[1]

This chapter begins with the observation, however, that this debate is but the latest manifestation of a long-standing tension in Australian foreign policy that reflects Canberra's cultural and historical ties to the Western world, juxtaposed against its geographic location on Asia's periphery. The chapter goes on to assess the arguments put forward by the two dominant camps in this debate. The first of those camps it characterises as the 'Crusaders', a collection of scholars and policy analysts who argue that Canberra needs to 'double down' on the American alliance going

---

1 See, for example, Brad Glosserman, 'The Australian Canary', *PacNet*, no. 67, Pacific Forum CSIS, 21 Nov. 2011.

forward with a view to seeing off the Chinese challenge to the US-led security order in Asia that has served Australia so well during the postwar period. The second it dubs the 'Pragmatists', a relatively diverse group who contend that Canberra needs to establish a greater degree of autonomy from Washington in a manner carefully calibrated to align with Asia's changing power dynamics. While successive Australian governments have essentially sought to have the best of both worlds by actively seeking and, by and large, achieving a remarkable degree of foreign policy autonomy within the bounds of the American alliance, the chapter concludes that this course is likely to become more challenging to maintain in the future as US expectations of Australia intensify in an increasingly contested Asia.

Torn Country

The most extensive reiteration of the debate regarding how Australia should position itself between China and America was initiated by the publication of Hugh White's 2010 *Quarterly Essay* 'Power Shift'.[2] White's work started out with the proposition that the US-led security order in Asia that had been in place since the end of World War II was coming under challenge in the face of China's rise. Whichever order replaced it, in White's view, would be an inherently more contested one. Given that such an outcome would not be in Australia's interests, White urged Australian policymakers to undertake a concerted effort to convince both Beijing and Washington to enter into a power-sharing arrangement—akin to that which operated reasonably effectively in Europe during the 19th century—rather than drifting into a dangerous strategic competition with considerable potential for war.[3] White also saw the need for India and Japan to be included in this arrangement, given that they are the region's other two major powers. At the heart of the power-sharing arrangement, however, was the fundamental need for Beijing and Washington to see one another as equals and to 'share power' in Asia on this basis. Should that outcome not eventuate, according to White, then Canberra would almost certainly be faced with an unenviable choice between its leading

2   Hugh White, 'Power Shift: Australia's Future between Washington and Beijing', *Quarterly Essay*, no. 39, Collingwood, Vic.: Black Inc, 2010.
3   For further reading on the Concert of Europe, see Carston Holbraad, *The Concert of Europe: A Study in German and British International Theory, 1815–1914*, London: Longman, 1970.

trading partner and its long-standing strategic ally, most dramatically in the case of conflict between these two heavyweights. In White's view, this was a choice best avoided.

The debate that White's work prompted is one with relatively deep historical roots. Indeed, Canberra has faced challenges regarding how to position itself between Beijing and Washington ever since the US–Australia alliance was conceived in the early 1950s. As Michael Wesley has observed, 'more than any other country, China has always symbolised for Australia the immanent evolution of the Asian regional order. This has been a nagging caveat in this country's deep commitment to, and investment in, the American-guaranteed global and regional orders'.[4] This observation is consistent with the late Samuel Huntington's famous characterisation of Australia as a 'torn country'—a people who, in his words, are 'divided over whether their society belongs to one civilization or another'.[5] Huntington here was referring to an Australia 'torn' between its cultural and historical ties with the Western world and its geographic proximity to Asia.

Washington very clearly required Canberra to make a choice between its history and its geography when it agreed to enter into a formal strategic alliance with Australia in the early 1950s. At the time, the Australian Foreign Minister, RG Casey, was actively considering an alternative multilateral organisation that would include not only his country's major power allies—Great Britain and the United States—but also the newly independent states of Asia. Even prior to that, the government under Ben Chifley was in 1949 seriously contemplating the possibility of following Britain's lead and formally recognising the newly established People's Republic of China (PRC) under Communist rule. After toying with and ultimately rejecting a prospective multilateral framework—akin to that which it had established in Europe following the ending of World War II[6]—Washington made clear to Canberra that in order to secure the alliance it sought so as to ease its anxieties regarding the prospect

4   Michael Wesley, 'Australia–China', in Brendan Taylor (ed.), *Australia as an Asia Pacific Regional Power: Friendships in Flux?*, London & New York: Routledge, 2007, p. 60.
5   Samuel P Huntington, *The Clash of Civilizations and the Remaking of World Order*, New York: Simon & Schuster, 1995, pp. 151–54.
6   For further reading, see Victor Cha, 'Powerplay: Origins of the US Alliance System in Asia', *International Security*, vol. 34, no. 3, Winter 2009/10, pp. 158–96. doi.org/10.1162/isec.2010.34.3.158.

of a remilitarised Japan, Australia needed to unequivocally support US policy in Asia. This included non-recognition of Communist China and forswearing any alternative Pan-Asian regional structures.[7]

Almost as soon as the ANZUS[8] Treaty had been signed, however, Canberra was testing Washington's limits in terms of how much leeway it would afford Australia as far as its China policies were concerned. Somewhat ironically, even as Australian troops were fighting against Chinese and Chinese-supported troops in the Korean War, Australia was already engaging in a burgeoning trading relationship with Communist China. By the early 1960s Australia had become China's leading supplier of wheat while, by the end of that decade, it was China's third-largest supplier of goods—second only to Japan and the then West Germany. Moreover, this was during a period when a US-led trade embargo was in place against Communist China—an instrument of economic statecraft that Canberra supported in relatively minimalist terms by adhering to the requirement it not supply Beijing with 'strategic materials'.[9]

By the early 1970s, daylight was again opening up between Canberra and Washington in their respective China policies, with Australia moving more quickly towards the formal normalisation of relations with Beijing than even the revolutionary diplomacy of the Richard Nixon and Henry Kissinger years. Gough Whitlam, leader of the opposition Australian Labor Party, for instance, led a delegation to Beijing in July 1971 only a matter of days before Kissinger famously visited there as US national security adviser. Whitlam was elected prime minister in the following year and one of his first acts was to formally recognise China in December 1972. He subsequently became the first Australian prime minister to visit the PRC in October 1973, during which time he was able to secure separate trade and technology agreements, coupled with the establishment of a joint trade committee. Most significantly in the context of the current chapter, however, all of this occurred in advance of the normalisation

---

7   Wesley, 'Australia–China', 2007, p. 62.
8   New Zealand was originally a member of the alliance, but its participation was suspended in 1986 following a dispute with the United States over the visits of nuclear ships. For further reading see Gerald Hensley, *Friendly Fire: Nuclear Politics and the Collapse of ANZUS*, Auckland University Press, 2013.
9   Wesley, 'Australia–China', 2007, p. 64.

of China–US relations in 1979. As Shannon Tow has thus observed, 'these milestones were hallmarks of an emerging Australia China policy that was less calibrated with Washington'.[10]

In perhaps the most direct antecedent to White's work, however, the former secretary of the Australian Department of Trade, Stuart Harris, published a monograph in the late 1990s titled simply *Will China Divide Australia and the US?*[11] While acknowledging that the China policies of Canberra and Washington had generally been fairly well aligned, Harris also pointed out that there had on occasion been quite public differences between them, particularly in relation to human rights issues. Moreover, Harris was also of the view that such differences were likely to become sharper and more pronounced in the future 'as the two countries accommodate, in their own responses to a changing regional environment, rising China'.[12] While predicting that Australia and America would continue to have common interests vis-à-vis China, Harris was also of the view that differences would open up due to their differing geography, geopolitical objectives, national interests and foreign policymaking processes. He suggested that these differences would grow in importance and that they had the potential to ultimately divide Canberra and Washington. His monograph was thus not only an attempt to identify these differences in advance, but also to develop effective strategies for managing them.

In some respects, the story of the US–Australia alliance during the period since Harris produced this monograph has been the antithesis of what he predicted. Writing recently in *Foreign Affairs*, for instance, Bates Gill and Tom Switzer argued that 'Australia now figures more prominently in US foreign policy than at any time since 1942–45, when Australian combat troops served under General Douglas MacArthur and scores of US air and naval bases and army camps were stationed Down Under'.[13] The alliance has unquestionably gone from strength to strength in recent years, deepening institutionally and broadening into new areas of cooperation such as cyber security, ballistic missile defence, space cooperation and new measures

---

10   Shannon Tow, 'Diplomacy in an Asymmetric Alliance: Reconciling Sino–Australian Relations with ANZUS, 1971–2007', *International Relations of the Asia-Pacific*, vol. 12, no. 1, 2012, p. 81. doi. org/10.1093/irap/lcr021.
11   Stuart Harris, *Will China Divide Australia and the US?*, Sydney: The Australian Centre for American Studies, 1998.
12   Harris, *Will China Divide Australia and the US?*, 1998, p. 1.
13   Bates Gill & Tom Switzer, 'The New Special Relationship: The US–Australia Alliance Deepens', *Foreign Affairs*, 19 Feb. 2015.

to combat terrorism. Of particular significance, during his first visit to Australia as president in November 2011, Barack Obama announced the establishment of the US Marine Corps Rotational Force, Darwin— this force will grow to 2,500 personnel in coming years and operate as a Marine Expeditionary Unit. Even more significantly, the 2014 Force Posture Agreement between the United States and Australia enabled not only the expansion of the US Marine Force, but also the rotation of a US Air Force presence in northern Australia including B-52 (and potentially B-1B) bombers, fighter jets and air-to-air refuelling aircraft.[14] Consistent with this, the Australian Government's 2016 defence white paper placed particular emphasis upon the acquisition of military capabilities that will enable Australian forces to operate in close cooperation with their American counterparts, particularly in South-East Asia.[15]

All of that said, however, differences between Canberra and Washington over China policy have also become more pronounced and more visible in recent years, precisely along the lines that Harris predicted. Perhaps the starkest example occurred in April 2015 when Australia opted to apply for membership of the Chinese-led Asian Infrastructure Investment Bank (AIIB). Canberra's decision was especially significant because it occurred in the face of strong and rather public opposition from the Obama administration. In October of the same year, further tensions were generated by the Australian Government's decision to grant a 99-year lease to Landbridge, a Chinese company with alleged links to the Chinese Communist Party (CCP). While the Australian Department of Defence had reportedly given the 'all clear' for this deal to go ahead, the Obama administration was reportedly disgruntled that it had not been consulted. Andrew Krepenivich summarised the mood in Washington at the time by suggesting that the Landbridge lease 'threaten[ed] to undermine Australia's relations with its closest security partner, the United States'.[16] As a consequence of this episode, coupled with Canberra's reluctance to adopt a stronger position in response to China's growing assertiveness in the South China Sea, reports soon emerged that Australian and American officials were engaged in 'emergency talks'.[17]

---

14   Greg Sheridan, 'B-1 Supersonic Bombers Coming to the North After All', *Australian*, 22 May 2015.

15   For further reading, see Peter Jennings, 'The 2016 Defence White Paper and the ANZUS Alliance', *Security Challenges*, vol. 12, no. 1, 2016, pp. 53–63.

16   Andrew Krepenivich, 'Darwin Port Deal with China's Landbridge Group an Unforced Error', *Australian*, 17 Nov. 2015.

17   Lisa Murray, 'US in Talks on Darwin Port', *Australian Financial Review*, 4 Dec. 2015.

The fact that such episodes were taking place against the backdrop of the debate sparked by White back in 2010 is by no means insignificant. It is a debate that has not gone unnoticed in Washington. Indeed, as two well-placed American commentators, Michael Green and Zack Cooper, observed in July 2015:

> for much of Australia's history, its leaders have been nervous about abandonment by its primary ally … In the midst of Asia's ascent today, however, it is Australians who worry about entrapment by Washington and Americans that worry about abandonment by Canberra.[18]

It is to the debate sparked by White in 2010 that this chapter now turns.

Crusaders

It is possible to characterise the various participants in the debate in a number of different ways. As will become apparent throughout the course of this chapter, there are also subtle variations *within*, as well as these clear differences between, the Crusader and Pragmatist camps.

Before proceeding to outline some of the primary contributions on either side of this debate, it is worth emphasising that the question at its centre is how much strategic autonomy Australia should exercise from the United States. To be sure, over the years a handful of scholars and analysts have suggested abandoning the American alliance altogether. The most recent example of this is a controversial book authored by former Australian prime minister, the late Malcolm Fraser.[19] In this book, Fraser characterises the alliance as a 'dangerous' strategic tie and one that critically inhibits Canberra's capacity to engage with its Asian neighbours. By and large, however, the vast majority of debate around the American alliance has not seriously considered the abandonment option. As Tow has observed, for instance, even the revolutionary Whitlam government of the 1970s was cognisant of this. In her terms:

---

18   Michael J Green, Peter J Dean, Brendan Taylor & Zack Cooper, 'The ANZUS Alliance in an Ascending Asia', *Centre of Gravity Series*, no. 23, Jul. 2015, p. 8.
19   Malcolm Fraser with Cain Roberts, *Dangerous Allies*, Carlton, Vic.: Melbourne University Press, 2014. For an earlier example of work calling for the complete abandonment of the American alliance, see David Martin, *Armed Neutrality for Australia*, Blackburn, Vic.: Dove Communications, 1984.

> Whitlam was acutely conscious that Sino–Australian relations should not develop at the expense of Australia's core strategic relationship with the United States. Although Whitlam is popularly represented as the harbinger of a more independent Australian foreign policy, he was acutely aware of Australia's strategic dependence on the American alliance.[20]

Those falling within the Crusader camp argue that, in a more contested Asia, Australia will not have the same luxury that those such as Whitlam have enjoyed in years gone by in terms of how much autonomy Canberra is able to exercise within the alliance. Instead, they argue that the very survival of the US-led security order in Asia, which has served Australia so well in the period since the end of World War II, is being fundamentally challenged as a direct result of China's growing power, influence and strategic ambition. In response to this challenge, Crusaders argue that Canberra needs to join American efforts to balance against China's rise. As Peter Jennings, Executive Director of the Australian Strategic Policy Institute (ASPI) and a prominent member of the Crusader camp, puts it:

> the strategic choice Australia faces is not the pulp fiction one of picking between the US and China. It's a choice about us: do we crouch or do we stand? Stand, that is, with a strong defence capability, a powerful alliance and a global network of friends. No choice at all, really.[21]

As Jennings' quote implies, these balancing efforts involve not only siding with the United States, but also coordinating much more closely with other American allies and partners to add further weight to Washington's position in Asia. There is a strong values-based logic underpinning such arguments, with Crusaders advocating closer collaboration between Canberra and other democratic partners and allies of America to preserve what Condoleezza Rice once famously characterised as a 'balance of power that favours freedom'[22] in the Asia-Pacific region. Andrew Shearer, another prominent member of the Crusader camp who served as a senior adviser to former prime minister Tony Abbott and who is now affiliated with the highly regarded Center for Strategic and International Studies (CSIS) in Washington DC, embraces this logic by encouraging 'the development of a network of like-minded partners who have both the political will and the capacity to contribute materially to maintaining a favourable balance

---

20   Tow, 'Diplomacy in an Asymmetric Alliance', 2012, pp. 81–82.
21   Peter Jennings, 'Australia Must Choose to Stand Tall in the Asia-Pacific Region', *Australian Financial Review*, 17 Feb. 2014.
22   The White House, Office of the Press Secretary, 'Dr Condoleezza Rice Discusses President's National Security Strategy', Waldorf Astoria Hotel, New York, 1 Oct. 2002.

of power in a rapidly changing region'.[23] Such arguments are consistently made by those in the Crusader camp to advocate closer strategic relations bilaterally between Australia and Japan, trilaterally to include Australia, Japan and the United States, and quadrilaterally by adding India into that mix.[24]

Unlike in the past, when Canberra has had little reluctance when it comes to issuing statements reflecting its strong rhetorical support for the American alliance, Crusaders also argue that Australia needs to undertake much more in the way of concrete action to actively support a strong US presence in a contested Asia. In recent months, such arguments have increasingly been made with reference to the South China Sea. This has been especially so since the United States began demonstrating its commitment to military overflight and freedom of navigation with respect to this body of water, as first evidenced by the October 2015 transit of the USS *Lassen* within 12 nautical miles of five features in the disputed Spratly Islands. As Ben Schreer and Tim Huxley, two prominent voices from the Crusader camp argued in the aftermath of this operation, 'words alone are not sufficient to stop China's maritime assertiveness. Expecting the US will somehow stand up to China on its own is a tall order. The cherished assumption that Australia can sail easily between China and the US is a flawed one'.[25] In a similar vein, following Beijing's February 2016 deployment of anti-aircraft missiles to Woody Island, Jennings argued that 'urging restraint and calm as prime ministers Malcolm Turnbull and New Zealand's [John] Key did last Friday is sensible enough, but realistically, the South China Sea issue is morphing from a dispute into a crisis. More is needed than soothing talking points'. Jennings then went on to propose:

> a better approach would be to strengthen and coordinate American and regional responses to China. This must include a shared, stronger, diplomatic response to Beijing and for a number of countries—not just the United States—to exercise military overflight and freedom of navigation manoeuvres.[26]

---

23   Andrew Shearer, 'Uncharted Waters: The US Alliance and Australia's New Era of Strategic Uncertainty', *Perspectives*, Lowy Institute for International Policy, Aug. 2011, p. 16.
24   See, for example, Andrew Shearer, 'Australia–Japan–US Maritime Cooperation: Creating Federated Capabilities for the Asia-Pacific', A Report for the CSIS Asia Program, Center for Strategic and International Studies, Washington DC, Apr. 2016.
25   Ben Schreer & Tim Huxley, 'Standing up To China is Essential, Even if Costly', *Australian*, 21 Dec. 2015.
26   Peter Jennings, 'South China Sea: We Should Push Back against New Drive', *Australian Financial Review*, 21 Feb. 2016.

Pragmatists

Juxtaposed against the Crusader camp, another school of thinking argues that Canberra should instead be seeking to distance itself somewhat from the alliance as Asia becomes more contested. There are a number of different variants of this argument. A particularly interesting feature of this line of thinking, however, is the significant number of former senior Australian politicians and officials who have associated themselves with the Pragmatist camp.

One notable example is former foreign minister Bob Carr, who argues that, by aligning itself too closely with the American alliance, Canberra risks entrapment within a conflict in which it has only peripheral interest. Carr has made this argument recently and publicly in relation to rising tensions around the East and the South China Seas disputes. To substantiate his arguments on the East China Sea, the Australia–China Relations Institute (ACRI), of which Carr is head, has undertaken polling of the Australian public showing that 71 per cent of Australians were against Australia taking sides in a conflict between China and Japan over the disputed Senkaku/Diaoyu Islands, whilst 68 per cent were of the view that the Australian Prime Minister should refuse any request from his American counterpart to provide military support in the event the United States were to become involved in any such contingency.[27] On the South China Sea, Carr contends that it would be a mistake for Canberra to follow the course suggested by the Crusaders with respect to so-called freedom-of-navigation operations given that few, if any, other Asian capitals would be willing to engage in these. In Carr's terms, 'do we want to be the only American friend, partner or ally to be donning a deputy sheriff's badge, glinting in the sunlight and running these sorts of patrols?'[28]

A second strand of the Pragmatist line of thinking argues that any decisive tilt towards the American alliance would be premature given the uncertain trajectory of the Sino–American relationship. According to this line of reasoning, while there will be competitive elements to this relationship in the foreseeable future, it is important not to underestimate the potential for Beijing and Washington to manage their differences and

---

27 Rowan Callick, 'Don't Take Sides in China–Japan Islands Conflict, Says Survey', *Australian*, 6 Jan. 2015.
28 'Australia Should Not Conduct "Missions" with US in South China Sea: Former FM', *Xinhua*, 4 Mar. 2016.

for the cooperative dimensions of the relationship to prevail. The classic statement from Canberra reflecting this logic can be found in the 2013 defence white paper, which stated:

> the Government does not believe that Australia must choose between its longstanding alliance with the United States and its expanding relationship with China; nor do the United States and China believe we must make such a choice.[29]

More recently, the recently retired Australian Secretary of Defence, Dennis Richardson, has continued to famously run a similar line. In Richardson's terms, 'our relationship with China and the United States can be summarised by one simple phrase: friends with both, allies with one'. Lest this be mistaken for a softer version of the Crusader line of argument, however, Richardson also places himself firmly within the Pragmatist camp by going on to observe that 'as close as we are to the United States, we do have our own interests and set our own course. Our relationship and interests in China are sometimes different to those of the United States'.[30]

A third strand of the Pragmatist school argues that, by distancing itself from Washington, Canberra stands the best chance of contributing—to the extent that a middle-sized power such as Australia possibly can— toward ameliorating deepening strategic competition between China and America. White's argument that Canberra should be urging Washington and Beijing to 'share power' in Asia places him squarely within this camp.[31] With specific reference to the South China Sea disputes, Wesley takes a similar line to White, arguing that Canberra needs to take a less timid approach in relation to these disputes and to draw inspiration from some of Australia's most activist diplomatic initiatives of days gone by—such as its promotion of a creative solution to the Cambodian conflict during the late 1980s and early 1990s—particularly given the considerable interests it currently has at stake in Asia. In Wesley's words:

---

29   Commonwealth of Australia, *Defence White Paper 2013*, Canberra: Department of Defence, 2013, p. 11.
30   Dennis Richardson, 'The 2015 Blamey Oration: The Strategic Outlook for the Indo-Pacific Region', 3rd International Defence and Security Dialogue, 27 May 2015, viewed 16 Jun. 2016, www.rusinsw.org.au/Papers/20150527B.pdf.
31   In addition to Hugh White's 2010 Quarterly Essay, see also Hugh White, *The China Choice: Why America Should Share Power*, Collingwood, Vic.: Black Inc, 2012.

were Washington to become embroiled in a conflict in the South China Sea, it is highly likely that Australia would be expected to fulfil its alliance obligations alongside US forces. Australia's acceptance as part of the Asia-Pacific region might also be challenged, a status that has been contested in the past and could be again in the future. An Australia that stands aloof from one of the region's key flashpoints could well be an Australia whose commitment to regional issues is questioned in future international relations.[32]

Trouble Ahead?

The voluminous scholarship on alliance politics has engaged surprisingly little with the issues surrounding the management of alliances. Instead, the focus of this work has been predominantly upon questions relating to the formation, persistence and collapse of these arrangements.[33] This is especially true of scholarship addressing Australia's alliance with America. In one of the few works to specifically address alliance management issues, however, the doyen of alliance politics Glenn Snyder points out that central to the task of managing any alliance, 'the parties will want to shape and control it so that it maximizes their net benefits'.[34] The analysis presented in this chapter suggests that, historically, Australia has certainly endeavoured to do so in its alliance with America, willingly accepting its characterisation as a 'Dependent' and 'Dependable' junior ally to the United States, but in practice actively seeking and successfully exercising a remarkable degree of independence within the bounds of this alliance relationship.

One could argue that Canberra has been able to exercise this degree of independence precisely because Washington has ultimately afforded it the luxury of doing so. Indeed, as detailed earlier in this chapter, after initially requiring Canberra to commit to US policy in the Asia-Pacific as a non-negotiable requirement for first entering into a formal alliance with America, Washington has generally during the period since afforded Canberra considerable latitude—especially so in its China policies—and has opted not to impose significant costs upon it, even in instances when

32 Michael Wesley, 'Timid Diplomacy Leaves Us in a Sea of Disputes', *Age* (Melbourne), 25 Sep. 2015.
33 See, for example, Stephan M Walt, *The Origins of Alliances*, Ithaca, NY: Cornell University Press, 1987.
34 Glenn H Snyder, *Alliance Politics*, Ithaca & London: Cornell University Press, 1997, p. 165.

Australia has clearly gone against the wishes of its senior ally, such as in April 2015 when Canberra applied for membership of the Chinese-led AIIB. Do outcomes such as these suggest that the Pragmatists are ultimately likely to prevail over the Crusaders in their ongoing debate as outlined in this chapter? Not necessarily.

Indeed, a case can be made that the future management of the American alliance may become more rather than less challenging and that history may not serve as a reliable guide for Canberra, particularly in an increasingly contested Asia. The noticeable degree of interest that Washington has paid to the Australian debate between the Crusaders and Pragmatists, for instance, points towards the possibility of an impending sea change in American attitudes towards the alliance. As Michael Green and Zack Cooper note, 'these public debates by the United States' closest ally in the Pacific have some senior US officials quietly questioning whether Japan may in future replace Australia as the most trustworthy ally should US and regional tensions continue mounting with Beijing'.[35] In the final analysis, therefore, while Australia's alliance with America is today in seemingly very good shape, as this relationship continues to both broaden and deepen and should Canberra expect to exercise the same degree of independence within the alliance that it has done historically, the task of managing its relations with Washington could well become more challenging and the potential costs associated with exercising such independence considerably greater.

35 Green, Dean, Taylor & Cooper, 'The ANZUS Alliance in an Ascending Asia', 2015, p. 7.

7

The Challenges and Dynamics of Alliance Policies: Norway, NATO and the High North

Wrenn Yennie Lindgren & Nina Græger

This chapter sets out to discuss two major framework conditions for Norwegian foreign, security and defence policy: North Atlantic Treaty Organization (NATO) and the High North.[1] Having to address increasingly heterogeneous security concerns and agendas, how do alliances shape their members' foreign, security and defence policies? And how do the specific challenges related to the High North, such as Russia and other states' policy agendas, form Norwegian responses and policies? In answering these questions, we aim to explore the framework conditions in a contemporary and historical context. Apart from contributing to the literature on Norway and NATO, we endeavour to add value to the general understanding of small states' foreign and security policy enablers and constraints.[2]

---

1   The term 'High North' (*nordområdene*) often appears in Norwegian Government documents and is used interchangeably with 'Arctic'. It does not refer solely to Norwegian territory, but is rather a broad concept that attempts to capture developments in the wider circumpolar area. See Jonas Gahr Støre, 'The High North and the Arctic: The Norwegian Perspective', *Arctic Herald*, Moskva, no. 2, Jun. 2012, www.regjeringen.no/no/aktuelt/nord_arktis/id685072/.
2   Christine Ingebritsen, 'Norm Entrepreneurs: Scandinavia's Role in World Politics', in Christine Ingebritsen, Iver Neumann & Sieglinde Gstohl (eds), *Small States in International Relations*, Reykjavik: University of Iceland Press, 2006, pp. 273–85; Anders Wivel, Clive Archer & Alyson JK Bailes, 'Setting the Scene: Small States in International Security', in Clive Archer, Alyson JK Bailes & Anders Wivel (eds), *Small States and International Security: Europe and Beyond*, London: Routledge, 2014, pp. 3–25.

As a small state located at NATO's northern flank, Norway has a keen interest in keeping the High North peaceful. Norway seeks predictability and stability in its relationship with its neighbours. Its sovereignty ultimately depends, however, on the maintenance of international law and order embedded in two elements. One is the international community and particularly the United Nations, which 'is Norway's first line of defence, literally speaking'.[3] The other is the alliance system and especially NATO's Article 5, and Norway's close bilateral relationship with the United States. A complicating factor is, however, that Russia–West/Russia–NATO relations often are reflected in and affect Norway's bilateral relationship with Russia in the High North—for instance, the bilateral relationship soured following Russia's intervention in Georgia.

In discussing the challenges and dynamics of Norway's alliance policy, this chapter focuses on three points in particular: first, what Norway as a country does to manage its security challenges and status as a small state, both through procurement policies and multilateral security cooperation; second, how Norway manages its relationship with its High North neighbour Russia; and, finally, to what degree Norway's 2014 Arctic policy and 2006 High North strategy have been adequate responses to the challenges above. The first two points mainly concern security, notably Norway's alliance policy (NATO membership), and bilateral relations with Russia. The final point, however, seeks to outline the room Norway has for pursuing a more independent yet inclusive foreign policy in the region to promote cooperation and competence sharing.

Russia has been a returning concern in both Norwegian and Western security discourses. From being an actor of limited resources that generated nominal interest in the 15 years after the Cold War ended, Russia has clearly re-emerged as an actor on the global scene. This has been felt both in the north, where the level of Russian military activity has increased considerably, but also in the south and the east, with the Russian interventions in Georgia (2008) and especially Ukraine (2014). The current threat from the Islamic State of Iraq and Syria (ISIS) and violent extremism, however, has ostensibly created the opportunity for a rapprochement between Russia and the West in the fight

---

3   Ministry of Foreign Affairs, *Interesser, ansvar og muligheter: Hovedlinjer i norsk utenrikspolitikk* (Interests, Responsibility and Possibilities: Approaches in Norwegian Foreign Policy), St. meld. 15 (2008–09), 13 Mar. 2009.

against terrorism. This recent move revisits questions about how to engage with Russia not only for NATO, but also in a local context, namely in the High North.

Overall, the bulk of existing literature on challenges in this region has been policy-specific, covering areas such as environmental policies, minority policies, fisheries, legal issues and energy extraction, including the role of big powers such as Russia, the United States and, potentially, China. Regarding Norwegian security, the literature has focused primarily on the challenges related to military developments in Russia and Russian intentions, as well as Norway's response in the form of military presence, exercises and surveillance of the seas. This essay contributes to the debate a discussion about how Norwegian policy has developed in light of an alliance that has to deal with increasingly diversifying—and at times diverging—security concerns and agendas, while at the same time having to deal bilaterally with Russia as a great power. To do so, we hone in on Norway's changing role in the alliance, as well as the alliance's role in and influence on Norway's defence policy. The handling of two intertwined priority areas of Norwegian foreign and security policy—Russia and the High North—is studied to demonstrate Norwegian approaches towards the challenges within the respective bilateral and multilateral contexts.

The chapter begins by contextualising Norway's current global position with a brief historical account of the country's foreign and security policy. Then we give an overview of Norway's historical alliance with the United States and NATO before embarking on a discussion of Norway as a notable defence spender and contributor to international security, challenging the view that Norway is a small state. The chapter proceeds with a discussion of how Norway manages its relationship with Russia bilaterally, but with a view to global security concerns. Finally, we analyse Norway's foreign policy options in the High North, a region that encompasses Norway's number one security policy focus area.

Norwegian Security and Defence Policy

Compared to its Nordic counterparts, Norway was a latecomer in developing its armed forces and independent foreign policy. This is largely due to the fact that Norway did not gain full independence until 1905. The country was under Danish rule for nearly 400 years before it was turned over to Sweden in 1814, after Denmark's loss in the Napoleonic wars. Norway declared itself neutral during World War I and maintained its neutrality until it was invaded by Nazi Germany in 1940. World War II was an instigator for change in Norway's defence and security policy. In the aftermath of the war, Norway developed its armed forces in line with its place in NATO's security strategy and with national defence concerns.[4]

Norway's NATO membership since 1949, with the concomitant binding guarantee of mutual security in Article 5 of the treaty, reinforced the promise of support in times of crisis. The Norwegian forces were dimensioned to deny an attacker the possibility of invading Norwegian territory or, if invaded, of putting up resistance (for 48 hours) until allies could come to Norway's assistance. Back then, as today, it was understood that 'assistance would have to come from the West, and it would have to be prepared in peacetime in order to be effective in times of war'.[5] Norway joined the alliance a year after turning down Sweden's 1948 proposition of a Scandinavian alliance and continues to hold that NATO defence cooperation is supreme over any other Nordic defence cooperation.[6] As we shall see, however, Norway does take part in security and defence cooperation with its Nordic neighbours (Nordic Defence Cooperation, NORDEFCO).

Norway's defence policy came to be based on the understanding that external support and reinforcement were an absolute necessity.[7] As an Atlantic coastal state with strong historical ties to the West, Norway has sought protection from Western great powers, in previous times particularly from the United Kingdom and, later, from the United States.[8] Having a close bilateral relationship with the United States was widely recognised in Norway as providing extra reassurance of the guarantee under NATO's Article 5. In addition to NATO membership, Norwegian defence against

4   Rolf Tamnes, *Norsk Utenrikspolitikks Historie, Bind 6, Oljealder 1965–1995*, Oslo: University Publisher, 1997; Kjetil Skogrand, 'Allierte i Krig og Fred 1940–1970' (Allied in War and Peace 1940–1970), vol. 4, *Norwegian Defence History*, Bergen: Eide Forlag, 2004.
5   Ministry of Defence, *Unified Effort*, Report of Expert Commission on Norwegian Security and Defence Policy, Norwegian Government, Jun. 2015, p. 14.
6   Ståle Ulriksen, 'Balancing Act – Norwegian Security Policy, Strategy and Military Posture', *Frivärld: Stockholm Free World Forum*, 2013, p. 5, viewed Aug. 2016, frivarld.se/rapporter/balancing-act-norwegian-security-policy-strategy-military-posture/.
7   Nina Græger, *Norsk Forsvarspolitikk: Fra invasjonsforsvar til internasjonal innsats 1990–2015* (Norwegian Defence Policy: From Invasion Defence to International Projection 1990–2015), Oslo: Spartacus forlag/Scandinavian Academic Press, 2016.
8   Nina Græger & Kristin M Haugevik, 'The Revival of Atlanticism in NATO? Changing Security Identities in Britain, Norway and Denmark', NUPI report, Oslo, 2009.

invasion was based on universal male conscription, mobilisation and total defence, where the whole society could be activated in case of an armed attack. Throughout the Cold War period, national defence was the main objective, with any international involvement a secondary task.[9]

The dissolution of the Soviet Union in 1991 and the realisation that the Russians were not about to invade only gradually changed Norway's security and defence policy. Change in the structuring of the armed forces took time but Norway did manage to transition to a post-national flexible defence.[10] This did not change the importance of NATO and Norway's close security relationship with the United States. But, in addition, the armed forces were transformed to meet the new international security environment and now participated in international peace operations, including peace enforcement operations. Around the year 2000, international operations were on par with national defence in Norwegian security concepts and strategies.

Preparing for an invasion over land became the main priority in post–World War II Norwegian security and defence policy. Consequently, the army was the lead service for Norway throughout the Cold War. Regarding international deployments, the Norwegian contributions to UN missions up until 1995—especially on the Korean peninsula, in the Gaza Strip and in Lebanon—were also mainly from the army. The air force played an important role in the air missions in Bosnia, Kosovo, Afghanistan (Operation Enduring Freedom) and Libya, and the navy participated in international missions in the first Gulf War, the Gulf of Aden and the Mediterranean. The army, however, has dominated Norway's long-term international engagements, as in Lebanon, the Balkans and Afghanistan (International Security Assistance Force, ISAF). Regarding territorial defence, however, the air force and the navy have arguably become lead services. Increased Russian military activity in the High North in more recent years has made both air surveillance and maritime security a higher priority on the Norwegian security agenda, as noted by the Defence Minister in 2014: 'Our vast ocean areas, and the resources that exist

---

9   Nina Græger, 'Home and Away? Internationalism and Territory in the Post-1990 Norwegian Defence Discourse', *Cooperation and Conflict*, vol. 44, no. 1, 2011, pp. 1–18. doi. org/10.1177/0010836710396347.
10   Ministry of Defence, 'Hovedretningslinjer for Forsvarets Virksomhet og Utvikling i Tiden 1999–2002' (Main Guidelines for the Armed Forces' Activity and Development in 1999–2002), White Paper no. 22, Oslo: Ministry of Defence, Norwegian Government, 1998; Ministry of Defence, *Kosovo-Krisen – Nasjonal rapport* (Kosovo Crisis – National Report), Norwegian Government, 24 Jan. 2001.

there, demand continuous presence and a robust capacity for surveillance, to maintain sovereignty and to exert authority.'[11] And, although the army remains important for territorial defence, a Russian invasion is unlikely in the foreseeable future.

Norway: A Standout Defence Spender and Participator

Many are puzzled by Norway's willingness to spend fortunes on defence material and capability contributions—in periods when most European NATO countries were and still are cutting defence budgets and investments, and despite its location in a part of the world experiencing relatively low tension.[12] Norway is a big spender within defence, spending more on defence per capita than any other European country. Over the years, Norway has maintained a relatively large defence budget and number of bases and installations across the country. In view of the post–Cold War security situation and with a large, expensive defence organisation, however, Norwegian political and military decision-makers were gradually convinced of the need to reform and downsize. More importantly, Norway needed to ensure interoperability with allied forces, as international operations in practice became the main task of the armed forces in the 1990s. With the global power shift and, especially, with Russia's more forward and aggressive foreign policy, defence budgets again became a cause for concern. Norway's defence budget has been stable and predictable and now amounts to some 43 billion Norwegian kroner, a 3.4 per cent increase compared with the core military budget for 2014.[13]

---

11   Ministry of Defence, 'Sikrer Ekstra Midler i år Til Kystvakten' (Secures Extra Funds to the Coast Guard this Year), Norwegian Government, 1 Feb. 2014, viewed Aug. 2016, www.regjeringen.no/no/aktuelt/kv-andenes-skal-repareres--sikrer-ekstra/id750283/.

12   Nina Græger, 'From "Forces for Good" to "Forces for Status"?: Small State Military Status-Seeking', in Benjamin de Carvalho & Iver B Neumann (eds), *Small State Status Seeking: Norway's Quest for International Standing*, Oxon and New York: Routledge, 2015, p. 101.

13   The costs of international deployments as well as procurement investments (e.g. the F-35s) are kept outside of the annual defence budget. See Ministry of Defence, 'Government Proposes 3.4% Defense Budget increase in 2015', Norwegian Government, 13 Oct. 2014, viewed Aug. 2016, www.regjeringen.no/en/aktuelt/Proposing-34-Defence-Budget-Increase-in-2015/id2005697/.

In 2015, the country ranked sixth worldwide on defence spending per capita, ahead of the United Kingdom and France.[14] The country's core defence budget is almost twice that of Denmark and Finland, and considerably bigger than Sweden's budget. Despite the NATO target that member states should each spend a minimum of 2 per cent of their national income or GDP on defence, few countries have been able to meet the target. At the NATO summit in Wales in September 2014, the ambitious target was replaced with the expectation that countries would halt any decline in defence expenditure.[15] Norway currently spends some 1.58 per cent of GDP and, although it will not meet the 2 per cent spending target, the proposed defence plan for the period 2017–20 suggests a substantial increase in total defence expenditure.[16] Given the drop in defence budgets in Europe, excluding the Baltics, Norway has put emphasis on the importance of greater self-reliance and it is expected that the defence budget will continue to be at the same level or increase.[17] Recent notable procurements in the defence sector have made estimates for a growing budget more likely. As pointed out by the Chief of Defence, however, 'to further today's economic framework implies that the Armed Forces will have to be further downsized'.[18] A returning issue has been Norway's propensity to spend large parts of the budget on operating expenses (e.g. maintenance), at the cost of investments in defence materials and installations or training, which strengthens the operational capability of the armed forces. Added to this is the fact that procurement costs have increased by some 4 per cent every year, which aggravates the situation.[19] This challenge is not unique for Norway and also holds for several NATO countries.

---

14   SIPRI, 'SIPRI Military Expenditure Database', *Stockholm International Peace Research Institute*, 2015.

15   North Atlantic Treaty Organization, 'Wales Summit Declaration', 5 Sep. 2014, viewed Aug. 2016, www.nato.int/cps/en/natohq/official_texts_112964.htm; Denitsa Raynova & Ian Kearns, 'The Wales Pledge Revisited: A Preliminary Analysis of 2015 Budget Decisions in NATO Member States', European Leadership Network, Feb. 2015.

16   Ministry of Defence, 'Kampkraft og bærekraft. Langtidsplan for forsvarssektoren' (Combat power and sustainability. Long term plan for the defence sector), Government Proposition 151 S (2015–16), Oslo: Ministry of Defence, Norwegian Government, 17 Jun. 2016.

17   SIPRI, 'Media Backgrounder: Military Spending in Europe in the Wake of the Ukraine Crisis', *Stockholm International Peace Research Institute*, 13 Apr. 2015.

18   The Armed Forces, *Et Forsvar i Endring* (A Defence Undergoing Change), Chief of Defence, 5 Oct. 2015.

19   Nils Holme, 'Forsvarspolitikken Ved et Veiskille' (Defence Policy at a Crossroad), Report, Oslo: Civita, 2013; see also, The Armed Forces, *Et Forsvar i Endring*, 2015.

Norway's relatively large defence expenses compared to most of its European allies have been reasonably distributed across the three branches of its defence: navy, air force and army. Starting with Norway's sea forces, being able to surveil the vast sea areas in the High North is central in the Norwegian defence concept and thinking.[20] A frigate procurement program was approved by the Norwegian Parliament in 1999 and completed over a decade later in 2011. The purchase of five Spanish-manufactured frigates was the biggest procurement expense in the history of the Norwegian navy.[21] Although the navy and the coast guard have made notable advances in capabilities and acquisitions over the past 10 years, training to develop the skills for using the new, advanced technologies has been under-financed. In the Cold War era, the navy was focused largely in the coastal areas to defend the littoral areas and sea lines of communication between northern and southern Norway and was in a constant state of high readiness. While the navy remains a coastal force today, it has increased seagoing capability and is especially working to reverse the drop in capabilities experienced during the Norwegian armed forces general 'low point' from 2008–12.[22] Most notably, in a series of acquisitions, a new logistics and support vessel is being made by South Korea.[23] This new acquisition will allow Norway to contribute on a higher level than it has in the past as the fleet is able to provide fuel, food, fresh water, ammunition and other supplies to other vessels around the world.[24]

Regarding special capacities, Norway is one of the few European states with a minesweeping capacity and a leader in European mine-warfare technology. In addition to the Royal Norwegian Navy's Oksoy- and Alta-class mine warfare vessels, the fleet has HUGIN Autonomous Underwater Vehicles provided by the Norwegian defence industry (Kongsberg Maritime). Further, Norway is in the process of upgrading its submarines after it was decided that the current Ula class would likely have life

20   Ministry of Defence, 'White Paper No. 1 (2012–2013) (2013 Budget)', presented to the Norwegian Parliament, 14 Sep. 2012.
21   Ministry of Defence, 'Future Acquisitions for the Norwegian Armed Forces 2014–2022', Norwegian Government, Mar. 2014, viewed Aug. 2016, www.regjeringen.no/globalassets/upload/fd/temadokumenter/acquisitions-2014-2022_mars-2014.pdf.
22   Ulriksen, 'Balancing Act – Norwegian Security Policy, Strategy and Military Posture', 2013.
23   Ministry of Foreign Affairs, 'Largest Ship of the Norwegian Navy Under Construction in South Korea', *Norway: The Official Site in South Korea*, 25 Jun. 2015, viewed Aug. 2016, www.navyrecognition.com/index.php/news/defence-news/year-2013-news/august-2013-navy-world-naval-forces-maritime-industry-technology-news/1191-south-koreas-dsme-wins-contract-for-design-and-build-of-a-new-logistics-support-vessel-for-norway.html.
24   Interview with employee in the Norwegian Navy, May 2015.

extensions until 2020 and then be replaced.[25] These submarines are viewed as a strategic deterrent by the Ministry of Defence[26] and are esteemed by experts to be Norway's strongest deterrent against military threats at sea.[27] The ongoing planning of the procurement of new submarines has reportedly involved discussion of possible joint scenarios with NATO partners Poland and the Netherlands, who are also in the process of planning their future procurements,[28] thus illustrating the international dimension of Norwegian procurement policy.

In addition to easing national concerns, these capacities enable Norway to participate actively in a multilateral context, also beyond NATO. Maritime surveillance and anti-piracy activities are two areas of particular Norwegian interest and involvement. Norway has participated in the European Union Naval Force—Operation Atalanta (EU NAVFOR), and in NATO's Operation Ocean Shield with vessels in the Gulf of Aden since 2008. Norway was also the first nation outside of Asia to join ReCAAP— the Regional Cooperation Agreement on Combating Piracy and Armed Robbery Against Ships in Asia, which works to fight pirates and other armed attacks against shipping in the Asian region, an important arena for Norwegian trade. It is also the only non-EU member of the Maritime Surveillance project (MARSUR), which was launched by the European Defence Agency in 2005 to create a network using existing naval and maritime information exchange systems.

Significant upgrades are also taking place in the Norwegian air force. The role of the Norwegian fighter plane fleet in the surveillance of the vast sea areas around Norway as well as responding to increased Russian air activity in the High North is essential.[29] The principle decision to replace the country's 52 F-16 fighter planes with 57 F-35 aircraft was approved by parliament in 2008, with the first training planes expected to be ready in 2017 and the remaining planes by 2020. As with the F-16s, the Norwegian Government opted for the US planes, to be manufactured by Lockheed Martin. In justifying the purchase, the government emphasised the excellence of the F-35s—as with the frigates before that—in surveillance

---

25 Ministry of Defence, 'Future Acquisitions for the Norwegian Armed Forces, 2014–2022', 2016.
26 Ministry of Defence, 'A Defence for Our Time', Government Proposition no. 73 (2011–12), presented to the Norwegian Parliament, 23 Mar. 2012.
27 Interview with employee in the Norwegian Navy, May 2015.
28 'Norway May Go Dutch with Poland on Subs', *Defence Industry Daily*, 10 Sep. 2015, viewed Aug. 2016, www.defenceindustrydaily.com/ula-tech-norways-next-submarine-fleet-07609.
29 Ministry of Defence, *Unified Effort*, 2015, p. 21.

and demonstration of sovereignty in the High North, as well as in combat (e.g. stealth capabilities) in international operations.[30] Apart from these qualities and the political prestige attached to the acquisition itself, these purchases signal to allies and partners that Norway is a country that takes responsibility for its own security, both nationally and globally.[31] Buying from American manufacturers also contributes to maintaining the close political bilateral relationship. In the 2017–2020 Long Term Defence Plan, the Chief of Defence emphasised national defence concerns and capacities aimed at protecting sovereignty, with the air force playing a central role.[32]

As a lead service during the Cold War, the Norwegian army was a priority in defence budgets. The army took the main cuts when the defence structure was downsized in the late 1990s and early 2000s and its main activity became, to a large extent, to be a provider of personnel to international operations. During 2003–14, the ISAF mission was its primary focus, as well as some other smaller operations. Defence spending related to the Norwegian army has mainly been directed towards lighter equipment, training and exercises, and operating expenses rather than procurement programs. The more forward-leaning Russian foreign policy posture is expected to upgrade the role of the army also in a national context. The proposed increased army presence in the two northern counties is, however, mainly a reallocation (*omdisponering*) of existing forces, not an increase in the total volume of army forces.[33]

Interoperability with NATO: The Role of Exercises

Close allies talk to and inform one another and work together, and are preferred partners. Participating in procurement programs, such as the Joint Strike Fighter program, connects Norway to NATO's most powerful member, both politically and militarily. Participating in the F-35 procurement program and the earlier F-16 program confirms—at least in Norway—the close and essential relationship with the United

---

30   Græger, 'Home and Away?', 2011.

31   Græger, 'Home and Away?', 2011.

32   This prediction is based on Fagmilitært råd (FMR), whose proposals are expected to be an essential input into the next defence plan.

33   The Armed Forces, *Et Forsvar i Endring*, 2015, p. 38ff.

States. Norwegian policy avers that it cannot take American interest for granted, and thus needs to work to keep the United States interested in the defence of Norway, also through force contributions—a policy that has not always been problem free.[34] According to the Norwegian Government, a strong transatlantic relationship is 'important not only for Norwegian security, but for the security of the entire Euro-Atlantic area and for global stability'.[35] In order to have this kind of partnership, forces need to be interoperable. Hence, Norwegian procurement policies and exercises are closely linked together.

Norway puts heavy emphasis on NATO joint exercises, especially on Norwegian soil, claiming that they ensure that NATO structures and forces are familiar with the Norwegian context (e.g. climate and terrain), interoperable and that the alliance's military capability is maintained and strengthened. Norway will be hosting a major NATO exercise in 2018, which the Defence Minister sees as 'Good [*Gledelig*] news for Norway and important for the Armed Forces'.[36] Procurement policies are also important for Norway's participation in NATO exercises beyond Norwegian territory. For instance, in summer 2014, Norway's Aegis frigate participated in the world's largest maritime exercise 'Rim of the Pacific', or RIMPAC, off Hawaii. Despite the existence of the exercise since the early 1970s, as Norway's first time participating, it was considered to have considerable strategic significance for the Norwegian defence community.

In June 2015, Norway participated in the annual, US-led Baltic Operations (BALTOPS) exercise, aimed at strengthening interoperability, capabilities and maintaining regional security. The exercise involved scores of ships and aircraft from 17 countries conducting naval drills in the Baltic Sea. Fourteen NATO allies were joined by NATO partners Finland, Georgia and Sweden, with 5,600 troops involved.[37] In January that year, Norwegian forces were among the 25,000 allied forces exercising together in a high-visibility exercise on the Iberian Peninsula that focused on crisis management. Furthermore, the North Atlantic

---

34   Græger, 'Home and Away?', 2011, p. 100.
35   Ine Eriksen Søreide, 'Speech at RIMPAC 2014 Seminar in Oslo May 12 2014', Minister of Defence, Ministry of Defence, 12 May 2014, viewed Aug. 2016, www.regjeringen.no/en/aktuelt/Speech-at-RIMPAC-2014-Seminar-in-Oslo-May-12-2014/id759104/.
36   Ministry of Defence, 'NATO Sier 'Ja' Til Stor-øvelse i Norge i 2018' (NATO Says 'Yes' to Major Exercise in Norway), Press Briefing no. 9/2015, Norwegian Government, 4 Feb. 2015.
37   Participants include Belgium, Canada, Denmark, Estonia, Finland, France, Germany, Georgia, Latvia, Lithuania, the Netherlands, Norway, Poland, Sweden, Turkey, the United Kingdom and the United States.

Council accepted Norway's offer to host the high visibility exercise in 2018, which, consistent with Norway's long-term efforts, will focus on collective defence. In her speech 'One for All, All for One', which refers to the security guarantee in Article 5, Defence Minister Ine Eriksen Søreide put a particular emphasis on the importance of collective self-defence for Norway and linked such exercises back to Norway's core concept.[38] Exercises are a reinforcement of Norway's alliance policy and close bilateral relationship with the United States. While welcoming the opportunity to raise the alliance's awareness of the north, however, Minister Søreide made the caveat that it was important to note that the exercise will benefit *all* allied and partner nations.[39]

The Norwegian Agenda in NATO

With regard to NATO, the Norwegian security and defence discourse is marked by a high degree of continuity. The defence of Norway is anchored in NATO's Article 5 and the close bilateral relationship with the United States, as noted above.

Norway has been an active member of NATO and has contributed to NATO activities and operations to maintain the mutual security guarantee and to ensure that the allies are likely to come to Norway's assistance in the event of an armed attack. To that end, the United States has pre-stocked military materials in Norway for quick access in times of crisis.[40] Furthermore, NATO's Joint Warfare Centre is located on the west coast in Stavanger, and has survived the many cuts of NATO presence (bases, installations) during the 1990s and 2000s. If, however, Norway was to find itself in a situation where NATO for some reason will not or cannot engage militarily, capable, modern and flexible Norwegian armed forces are necessary. This argument was key when seeking domestic support from the general public and the military for the transformation of the armed forces from a static territorial defence into a more flexible tool, both.[41]

---

38   Ine Eriksen Søreide, 'Speech by Ine Eriksen Søreide: "One for All, All for One"', Minister of Defence, Norwegian Government, 18 Mar. 2015, viewed Aug. 2016, www.regjeringen.no/en/aktuelt/speech-by-ine-eriksen-soreide-one-for-all-all-for-one/id2401315/.
39   Søreide, 'Speech by Ine Eriksen Søreide: "One for All, All for One"', 2015.
40   Preparedness in the event of an attack on Norway or other allies is also a NATO concern. According to the 2015 Expert Commission's report: 'NATO is in the process of clarifying command and control relations between NATO and national command structures in the event of crisis and war' (Ministry of Defence, *Unified Effort*, 2015, pp. 40–41).
41   Græger, 'Home and Away?', 2011, p. 100.

Being able to offer relevant and capable forces is also important to fulfil Norway's role and commitments as a NATO member. In terms of military assets, for a small country, Norway pulls above its weight. Through its procurement policy and deployments to international operations, Norway has also sought influence, status and recognition in NATO and other important fora, and vis-à-vis central allies, a strategy that has been referred to as a 'troops-for-influence' policy[42] and a 'forces-for-status' policy.[43] All of these practices may accord Norway a special status with the United States, which potentially enhances Norway's status inside NATO as well as its security, as Nina Græger points out.[44] In addition to contributing beyond the expectations of a state of its size, this also enables Norway to follow the moves of its neighbour closely, in the interest of both domestic and international security. This puts into question the extent to which this relatively high defence spending also enables a more independent direction in its foreign policy, and in the region, as we shall see below.

Regarding NATO policies, the primary input from Norway in the most recent strategic concept process was the 'Core Area Initiative', a 'non-paper' issued in 2008. The need to establish a better balance between NATO's engagement at home and abroad was a—if not *the*—major concern in Norway's views on and input into the strategic concept revision process during 2008–10.[45] Norway was not alone in expressing concerns about powerful neighbours and putting forward a call for the need to review NATO's strategy in light of the new developments, which were supported by the Eastern European members. The main message of the Norwegian initiative was that NATO should focus on and direct its training and exercises more towards its core tasks (e.g. Article 5) and the challenges in its neighbourhood to balance the out-of-area operations that had become NATO's main priority since the mid-1990s.[46] Regarding national defence responses, the concerns about Russian foreign policy were reflected in the concept of 'threshold (or literally "doorstep") defence'.[47]

42   Nina Græger, 'Norway and the EU Security and Defence Dimension: A "Troops-for-Influence" Strategy', in Nina Græger, H Larsen & H Ojanen, *The EDSP and the Nordic Countries: Four Variations on a Theme*, Programme on the Northern Dimension of the CFSP, Helsinki & Berlin: Ulkopoliittinen instituutti & Institut für Europäische Politik, 2002, pp. 33–89.

43   Græger, 'Home and Away?', 2011, pp. 91–92.

44   Græger, 'Home and Away?', 2011, p. 100.

45   Jakub Godzimirski, Nina Græger & Kristin M Haugevik, *Towards a NATO à la Carte? Assessing the Alliance's Adaptation to New Tasks and Changing Relationships*, NUPI Report, 2010.

46   Græger, 'Home and Away?', 2011, p. 15.

47   Ministry of Defence, 'White Paper No. 1'; Ministry of Defence, 'A Defence for Our Time', 2012.

NATO's response to the Ukraine crisis evolving in 2014 demonstrates that the majority of NATO countries now support a rebalancing between deterrence and international operations. NATO's Readiness Action Plan – which is 'the biggest reinforcement of NATO's collective defence since the end of the Cold War', according to NATO secretary general Jens Stoltenberg—was unveiled at the 2014 NATO summit in Wales.[48] The plan is composed of two pillars: immediate 'assurance measures' and longer-term 'adaptation measures'. Assurance measures focus on increased activity for assurance and deterrence and involve immediate reinforcements of alliance presence in the eastern part of the alliance to increase readiness in the area. Adaptation measures, which are still under implementation, involve longer-term changes to the alliance's force posture and its capabilities to respond more quickly to emergencies.[49] As part of the assurance measures, Norway (along with Belgium, Italy and the United Kingdom) assumed responsibility for air-policing duties as of 1 May 2015. Norway is also part of the UK-led Framework Nation Concept (FNC) initiative—a Joint Expeditionary Force (JEF) that also includes the Netherlands, Denmark, Estonia, Latvia and Lithuania. The JEF is set to deploy rapidly into theatre, particularly in the Baltic region, to conduct the full spectrum of operations, and to increase alliance readiness and ability to project maritime and amphibious power in the North and Baltic Seas.[50] Regarding its timeline, the United Kingdom intends to integrate JEF partners' contributions fully into the UK's existing high-readiness capabilities before 2018.[51] In the Norwegian view, the JEF and other initiatives within the Readiness Action Plan, as well as later decisions and follow-up measures at the Warsaw NATO Summit in July 2016, build on the same ideas that were forwarded in the 2008 Core Area Initiative, namely that the alliance should put its emphasis on its periphery over out-of-area operations.

The Alliance's strategic shift of focus to the Baltic Sea region and eastern NATO members, which occurred from northern fall 2014 to northern spring 2015, has been described by various scholars as a 'new normal'

---

48   NATO, 'NATO's Readiness Action Plan: Factsheet', Dec. 2014, p. 1.
49   NATO, 'NATO's Readiness Action Plan: Factsheet', May 2015, p.1.
50   Xavier Pintat, 'NATO's Readiness Action Plan: Assurance and Deterrence for the Post-2014 Security Environment', Sub-committee on Future Security and Defence Capabilities, NATO Parliamentary Assembly, 21 Aug. 2015, pp. 7–8.
51   Pintat, 'NATO's Readiness Action Plan', 2015.

for cooperative security.[52] Despite their non-NATO status, both Sweden and Finland have stepped up cooperation with alliance members, on multilateral and bilateral levels, intensifying debates about full membership.[53] Impetus for this shift and the development of the 'new normal' contextualisation came in the form of repeated Russian military activity in the Baltic Sea region, where Russian air activity—including heavy strategic bombers—tripled during 2013–14.[54] The activity also includes incursions into Nordic and Baltic air space and the newsworthy, intensive submarine incident in Sweden in October 2014.[55] Finnish and Swedish NATO membership debates also intensified when Russia conducted a big military exercise where the scenario allegedly was a rapid intervention in the islands of Åland (Finland), Gotland (Sweden), Bornholm (Denmark) and northern Norway.[56]

Norway, Russia and the 'Dual Policy' Tradition

As mentioned in this chapter's introduction, Norway–NATO relations and Norway–High North issues are somewhat inseparable. Due to geography, Norway–High North issues naturally involve Norway's bilateral relations with Russia. In addition, as Nina Græger argues: 'A complicating element is that this relation is not only defined by bilateral relations but also mirrors the temperature in the relationship between Russia and the West.'[57] Tuomas Forsberg and Græme Herd (2015) suggest

---

52   Anna Wieslander, 'A New Normal for NATO and Baltic Sea Security', UI Brief, no. 2, 2015; Søreide, 'Speech by Ine Eriksen Søreide: "One for All, All for One"', 2015.

53   See for instance Erik Brattberg & Henrik Breitenbauch, 'Time for Sweden to Join NATO', *The American Interest*, 25 Jun. 2015. For discussion on Swedish and Finnish policy towards engagement in NATO, see Hannah Ojanen, 'Finland's Relation with NATO in the Shadow of Russia', Cicero Foundation Commentary no. 14/03, Sep. 2014.

54   The Armed Forces, *Et Forsvar i Endring*, 2015, p. 15.

55   Aylin Matlé & Alessandro Scheffler Corvaja, 'From Wales to Warsaw: A New Normal for NATO?', *Fact and Findings: Prospects for German Foreign Policy*, no. 187, Oct. 2015; as also picked up in Ministry of Defence, *Unified Effort*, 2015, p. 5. In the Nordic context, military cooperation is generally organised under NORDEFCO (Nordic Defence Cooperation).

56   George Lucas, 'The Coming Storm: Baltic Sea Security Report', Center for European Policy Analysis, Washington DC, Jun. 2015, viewed Aug. 2016, www.cepa.org/sites/default/files/styles/medium/Baltic%20Sea%20Security%20Report-%20(1).compressed.pdf.

57   Nina Græger, 'Norges Sikkerhetspolitiske Instrumenter – Utfordringer og Muligheter' (Norway's Security Policy Instruments – Challenges and Possibilities', in Pernille Rieker & Walter Carlsnaes (eds), *Nye Utfordringer for Europeisk Sikkerhetspolitikk. Aktører, Instrumenter og Operasjoner*, Oslo: University Printing, 2009, p. 151.

that the increasingly aggressive Russian foreign policy, since 2014 in particular, marks a new low in NATO–Russia relations.[58] In his preface to the annual report on NATO activity in 2015, Stoltenberg emphasised restoring predictability to the alliance's relationship with Russia: 'There is no contradiction between increasing the strength of NATO and engaging Russia. Indeed, it is only by being strong that we can develop a cooperative and constructive relationship.'[59] Stoltenberg also stressed this strategy in his inaugural speech in 2014, pointing to his experience with managing bilateral relations with Russia during his 10 years as Norwegian prime minister.[60]

Although Russia is perceived by Norway to be an important and demanding neighbour, Norway remains committed to engaging Russia through its so-called 'dual policy' tradition, which focuses on mutual cooperative interests. For instance, the tradition, which was especially evident from the mid-1970s, instigated closer Norway–USSR cooperation on fisheries management during the Cold War, where the precautionary approach was key.[61] As pointed out by the Norwegian Expert Commission on Norwegian Security and Defence Policy:

> There is no contradiction between a distinct policy of firm line-drawing toward Russia and active collaboration. Norway has a long tradition of using this dual policy. As long as Russia's orientation is considered to be interest-based, co-operation will be possible when deemed useful to both parties. Therefore, in difficult periods our policy towards Russia must be based on strategic patience.[62]

Defence Minister Søreide confirmed Norway's post–Crimea implementation of the dual policy in a March 2015 speech stating that, although Norway suspended bilateral military cooperation with Russia in light of the unilateral annexation of Crimea, it continued day-to-day practical collaboration in coast and border guard activities and search and rescue operations, and cooperation regarding the Incidents at Sea

---

58   Tuomas Forsberg & Græme Herd, 'Russia and NATO: From Windows of Opportunities to Closed Doors', *Journal of Contemporary European Studies*, vol. 23, no. 1, 2015, p. 41.

59   NATO, *The Secretary General's Annual Report 2015*, 28 Jan. 2016, pp. 7, 10, www.nato.int/cps/en/natohq/opinions_127331.htm.

60   NATO, 'NATO: A Unique Alliance with a Clear Course', 28 Oct. 2014, www.nato.int/cps/en/natohq/opinions_114179.htm?selectedLocale=en.

61   Ministry of Defence, *Unified Effort*, 2015, pp. 71–72; Geir Hønneland, *Making Fishery Agreements Work: Post-Agreement Bargaining in The Barents Sea*, Cheltenham and Northampton, MA: Edward Elgar, 2013.

62   Ministry of Defence, *Unified Effort*, 2015.

Agreement. An open line between the respective countries' national Joint Headquarters and the Northern Fleet is also maintained to avoid misunderstandings or miscalculations.[63] Reassuring Russia through transparency and open lines has been a main strategy for Norway throughout the Cold War and during later incidents, such as the Russian invasion of Georgia in 2008.

A particularly important civilian arena is the Barents Secretariat, which involves all the countries in the Northern Hemisphere.[64] In the bilateral relationship, cooperation in civilian policy areas—such as fisheries, minority issues (especially regarding the indigenous Sami people), as well as people-to-people exchanges facilitated by the 2012 visa-free crossings agreement[65]—have allowed for ongoing communication and collaboration. However, bilateral cooperation in the management of the stream of refugees coming into Norway over the Russian–Norwegian border in the north (at Storskog) has been a mixed experience.[66]

Norway's Stakes in the High North

As a country with more than 80 per cent of its sea territory and 40 per cent of its land territory located north of the Arctic Circle, the High North is an area of deep interest for Norway. Under the 1920 Svalbard Treaty (Spitsbergen Treaty), Norway's sovereignty over the Svalbard archipelago is formally recognised and supported by the 40 High Contracting countries. The High North is also an area of change occurring on environmental, economic and geopolitical levels. Constant physical fluctuations in the region require close monitoring, the identification and separation of short- and long-term policy approaches and preparedness for potential

---

63   Søreide, 'Speech by Ine Eriksen Søreide: "One for All, All for One"', 2015.
64   The International Barents Secretariat facilitates multilaterally coordinated activities between the Barents Euro-Arctic Council (BEAC) and the Barents Regional Council. BEAC members include Denmark, Norway, Finland, Iceland, Sweden, Russia and the European Commission. The Norwegian Barents Secretariat focuses on developing Norwegian–Russian relations through funding for bilateral collaborative projects on behalf of the Norwegian Ministry of Foreign Affairs.
65   Heather Yundt & Catherine Benesch, 'Visa-free Agreement Sign of Strong Border Relationship', *Barents Observer*, 29 May 2012, barentsobserver.com/en/borders/visa-free-agreement-sign-strong-border-relationship.
66   Alissa De Carbonnel, 'A (Very) Cold War on the Russia–Norway Border', *Foreign Policy*, 20 Nov. 2015, foreignpolicy.com/2015/11/20/a-very-cold-war-on-the-russia-norway-border-syrian-refugees-bicycles/; Verdens Gang, 'Russland stanser asyl-returer over Storskog' (Russia Stops Asylum Returns over Storskog), 23 Jan. 2016, www.vg.no/nyheter/innenriks/flyktningkrisen-i-europa/russland-stanser-asyl-returer-over-storskog/a/23601737/.

crisis situations.[67] According to the Norwegian Foreign Minister, Børge Brende, the High North constitutes Norway's most important strategic area of responsibility, where Norway promotes a cooperative framework to responding to the changes taking place.[68] Internationally, Norway has been recognised as an international relations entrepreneur in the Arctic.[69] This means that Norway has sought to distinguish itself through a role as a 'convenor' in Arctic affairs—bringing together different kinds of actors and interests—and also as a 'bridge builder', especially in assisting other countries in their relationship to and understanding of Russian northern policy.[70]

The extent of Norway's interest in the maritime domain is vast and covers several fields, including fishing, transport, official supply services, deep sea services, drilling seismic oil and gas. Nearly 90 per cent of Norway's export revenues come from sea-based economic activity and resources. As a country that lives off of the sea, Norway's maritime approach is pragmatic: to keep the sea lanes open and to defend the country's rights. This is because its livelihood is dependent on the ocean and its resources. The report from the Expert Commission on Norwegian Security and Defence Policy reiterates the statement from the Ministry of Foreign Affair's white paper on the main guidelines in Norwegian foreign policy, emphasising the role of the international community and international law for Norway's safety:

> A robust international framework is important for Norway. Especially for small countries, it is essential that the great powers recognise the importance of common rules of the game and do not threaten the system's existence. In the same way, it is important to maintain international rule of law, institutions, regulations and norms that regulate behaviour and contribute to conflict resolution. The UN should continue to play a central role in this system. As a major maritime state, Norway draws heavily on the global regulations at sea including the UN Convention on the Law of the Sea of 1982, UNCLOS, as constitution of the seas.[71]

---

67   Katarzyna Zysk & David W Titley, 'Signal, Noise and Swans in Today's Arctic', *The SAIS Review of International Affairs*, vol. 35, no. 1, 2015, p. 177.
68   Børge Brende, 'The Arctic: Important for Norway, Important for the World', *Harvard International Review*, vol. 36, no. 3, 16 Apr. 2015, hir.harvard.edu/the-arctic-important-for-norway-important-for-the-world/.
69   Geir Hønneland & Lars Rowe, *Nordområdene – hva nå?* (The High North – What Now?), Trondheim: Tapir Academic Press, 2010.
70   Elana Wilson Rowe, 'Arctic Hierarchies? Norway, Status and the High North', *Polar Record*, vol. 50, no. 1, 2014, pp. 72–79. doi.org/10.1017/S003224741200054X.
71   Ministry of Defence, *Unified Effort*, 2015, p. 14.

Engaging the United States in the High North is an area of interest for the Norwegian Government. Cultivating American interest in the region has coincided with efforts to strengthen northern European defence cooperation, as broader and closer cooperation is believed to enhance security of the region on various levels.[72]

High North, Low Tension?

Whereas the end of the Cold War implied that 'for most other states than Russia the region has remained either marginal or peripheral', the importance of the High North was revitalised in Norway with the Norwegian High North strategy from 2005 onwards.[73] The significant Russian military build-up on the Kola Peninsula from the mid-2000s also raised concerns about security among Norwegian politicians, diplomats and militaries. In particular, the Russian reopening of old military bases, the increased level of military exercises and, not least, the increase in overflights of Russian bombers and strategic bombers off the coast of Norway sparked a new round of 'New Cold War' rhetoric and media headlines.

Certainly, a more aggressive Russian foreign policy towards Eastern Europe and Ukraine in 2014 in particular has also put the High North, where Russia has 'geo-political and military-strategic interests', back at the top of the Norwegian security and defence policy agenda.[74] For instance, the main focus of the expert commission was the security challenges that Russia represents in the region, which they describe as 'an arena for geopolitical struggle'.[75] The forward-leaning Russian foreign policy has also gained a lot of attention in Nordic academic environments.[76] Even after the Ukraine crisis, however, Russia has not been considered as a direct threat to Norway, at least not at present.[77] As formulated by the head of Norwegian military intelligence, 'Russia has not suddenly

---

72 Ministry of Defence, *Unified Effort*, 2015, p. 42.
73 Græger, *Norsk Forsvarspolitikk*, 2016, pp. 231–32.
74 Ministry of Defence, *Unified Effort*, 2015, p. 15.
75 Ministry of Defence, *Unified Effort*, 2015, p. 14.
76 See, for example, Forsberg & Herd, 'Russia and NATO', 2015; Jo Georg Gade & Paal Sigurd Hilde, 'Nordområdenes sikkerhetspolitiske betydning for NATO' (The High North's Security Policy Importance for NATO), in Tormod Heier & Anders Olav Kjølberg (eds), *Norge og Russland. Sikkerhetspolitiske utfordringer i nordområdene* (Norway and Russia. Security Policy Challenges in the High North), Universitetsforlaget, 2015, pp. 96–109.
77 Ministry of Defence, *Unified Effort*, 2015, p. 15.

become a military threat—not in the short term. But, in the long term the picture is more uncertain'.[78] Hence the focus on strengthening the military presence in northern Norway in subsequent defence plans and reports.[79] Rather than seeing any impending security threats in the region, the Norwegian Ministry of Foreign Affair's Arctic slogan, 'high north, low tension', emphasises the safety aspect of Arctic activity.

All of the peacetime, cooperative military bilateral and multilateral arrangements in the Arctic are between the nation states in the region. For instance, the Ilulissat Declaration of 2008, signed by the five Arctic coastal states, established a common framework for maritime sovereignty in the Arctic Ocean. All signatories have agreed that claims and disputes are to be negotiated between the Arctic coastal states to prevent the escalation of political disagreements into security issues. Norway and Russia, who have had overlapping claims in the Barents Sea for decades, finally managed to conclude negotiations and sign an agreement in 2010.

The role of NATO in the region has been brought up from time to time. NATO is not, however, likely to increase its activity in the Arctic in peacetime and instead encourages the continuation of the cooperation between all of the Arctic states. The defence establishments of the Arctic states promote peacetime confidence-building measures.[80] There are regular bilateral and multilateral military exercises in the region that include Russia and the individual NATO members among the Arctic states. There are annual informal meetings between military leaders from all of the Arctic states where 'soft security' measures and military support to civilian agencies responsible for safety-related matters are discussed. These matters have become increasingly important with growing levels of human activity in the Arctic Ocean. This emphasis on safety capabilities corresponds with recent efforts under the auspices of the Arctic Council that resulted in a new search and rescue agreement (2011) and an oil-spill preparedness and response agreement (2013).

The requirement for monitoring and safety arrangements depends on the volume and scope of future civilian activities. The Arctic may be a promising area for commercial opportunities. There is a potential

78 Forsvarets Forum, 'Nabovarsel' (Neighbour Warning), 25 Feb. 2015, p. 27.
79 For example, *The Strategic Military Review* (Fagmilitært råd, FMR), which is the armed forces' own recommendation to the politicians on how the organisation should evolve in the coming years (The Armed Forces, *Et Forsvar i Endring*, 2015).
80 This refers to the respective national governments' as well as alliance memberships.

for shorter transcontinental maritime transit though the Northern Sea Route, increasing the profit and value of extraction of onshore and offshore petroleum and mineral resources. Analysts, however, have recently addressed several factors dampening the most optimistic future predictions. Operations in the Arctic environment can be complex, difficult (extremely low temperatures and icing contribute to this) and costly. Profitability of commercial ventures in the Arctic may also be influenced by the dynamics in the market itself and evolving concepts for production and distribution.

The Arctic—where Norway has invested significant political and economic capital—can be seen as a unique arena for the country as a place where Norway meets and interacts with many non-Arctic states. Meeting both Arctic and non-Arctic partners in the High North has been a priority for Norway. For instance, the rapidly growing economies of Asia have expressed a particular interest in the Arctic, which has coincided with Norway's recognition of Asia as an increasingly important arena for Norwegian foreign policy.[81] Similar to its other Nordic regional partners, Norway has been forthcoming and welcoming of Asian states' Arctic interests, as it encourages broad dialogue on issues affecting the Arctic and competence sharing. Norway welcomes the diverse opinions, complementary expertise and outside-of-the-Arctic thinking that non-Arctic states can provide. Norway has developed especially close bilateral ties on Arctic issues with Singapore, South Korea and Japan. South Korea has prioritised Norway as a cooperation partner in Arctic and regular bilateral interactions between Norway and Singapore and Norway and South Korea have also strengthened collaborative commitments and interest in the region.[82] Norway proclaimed its support of the Asian states' inclusion in the Arctic Council in early 2013 and continued to play a role in the states' ultimate acceptance and inclusion in the council's ministerial meeting in Kiruna, Sweden, in May 2013. This receptive attitude towards the Asian states can be in part explained by a Norwegian interest in revitalising the Arctic Council.[83] Given its geographic placement and record in the High North,

---

81   Ministry of Foreign Affairs, 'Largest Ship of the Norwegian Navy', 2015.
82   Børge Brende, 'Cooperation between Norway and the Republic of Korea in a Changing Arctic Landscape', Norwegian Minister of Foreign Affairs, 2015.
83   Per Erik Solli, Elana Wilson Rowe & Wrenn Yennie Lindgren, 'Coming into the Cold: Asia's Arctic Interests', *Polar Geography*, vol. 36, no. 4, 2013, p. 262. doi.org/10.1080/108893 7X.2013.825345.

Norway can play a significant role as a gatekeeper and facilitator of non-Arctic states' interests in the region, which can in turn have positive offshoots in other bilateral, regional and international settings.[84]

Conclusion

Norway is a country where security and defence are core policy areas and political concerns. It has a well-funded national defence, relatively speaking, but one that is also committed to resolving disputes peacefully, and places great importance on security cooperation and its alliances. Since the first line of defence will often be abroad for small countries like Norway, it recognises the importance of maintaining an international order based on international law and the United Nations. Norway's contributions to NATO operations and important coalitions of the willing, and close bilateral relationship with the United States are also key in this respect. Here, Norway's procurement policy and willingness to contribute to peace operations as well as military enforcement operations around the world has placed it among the preferred allies in the past few years. This is a policy that has not only been conducted for the sake of status and recognition in NATO, but also to signal that Norway is no longer only an importer of security (having anchored its security in NATO's Article 5 since 1949). Given the country's positioning and that its maintenance of international law and order, support of the UN, and enforcement and exercises of sovereignty are major areas of national defence focus, Norway is increasingly also an *exporter* of security.

The challenges and dynamics inherent in Norway's alliances have led to policy approaches and acquisitions that further commitments beyond Norwegian borders. Norway's participation over the years in expensive procurement programs and ambition not only to participate in but also to host international—and especially NATO—exercises is a testament to the importance of its outward-looking and alliance-anchored security and defence policy. It is also a reflection of raised domestic and allied security concerns related to a more aggressive Russian foreign policy, as well as 'new threats' from terrorism, cyber attacks and 'hybrid warfare'. For a small country located on the outskirts of Europe, the importance of international law and order cannot be overemphasised. This does not,

---

84   Solli, Rowe & Yennie Lindgren, 'Coming into the Cold', 2013.

however, stand in contrast to having a flexible and modern defence, but rather coincides with it. The general concern expressed by several defence ministers over the past decade is the dilemma of facing a situation where a given conflict is too small for NATO, yet too large for Norway to handle alone, or at a point in time where NATO is engaged elsewhere. Consequently, and in response to recent aggressive Russian foreign policy and military build-up, Norway is reallocating and strengthening its military presence in the northern part of the country.

In the High North, Norway is recognised for its entrepreneurial and inclusive approach towards the states and entities involved, as well as its dedication to the maintenance of a safe and predictable Arctic environment and the resolution of disputes in a peaceful, law-abiding manner. Norway's pragmatic dual-policy tradition toward its Russian neighbour has allowed for steady communication and collaboration both in times of war and peace and at various levels of society. Although the long-term outcome of Russia's increasingly strong defence posture is uncertain, at present Russia is not considered to be a direct threat for Norway. With NATO activity in the Arctic unlikely to increase, the continuation of cooperation between the Arctic states through confidence-building measures remains a top foreign policy priority for Norway as it navigates the challenges and dynamics of its modern alliance structures and policies.

NATO, and thus Norway, faces an increasingly complex security environment defined by indiscriminate international terrorism, an unprecedented refugee crisis and a more assertive and unpredictable Russian military posture. With the alliance's primary focus on its core tasks of collective defence, crisis management and cooperative security, Norway's reputation as a defence spender and its extended role as an exporter of security is likely to remain a source of assurance both on bilateral and multilateral levels.

8

An Ally at the Crossroads: Thailand in the US Alliance System

Kitti Prasirtsuk

In the second decade of the 21st century, the United States is increasingly finding itself in a difficult situation on several fronts. The economic turbulence ushered in by the Subprime Crisis of 2008 led to long-term adverse effects on the US economy. This economic crisis has signified the relative decline of Western supremacy, as the economic difficulties have been lengthy and particularly spread to the Eurozone, the recovery of which is even more delayed than that of the United States. In terms of security, the War on Terror turned out to be a formidable threat, as demonstrated in the form of extremist terrorism wrought under the banner of Islamic State of Iraq and Syria (ISIS), which is now involving more people and is spreading beyond the Middle East. Europe's immigrant crisis is also giving the West a headache. The rise of China insists that the United States has to recalibrate its strategy in managing allies and partner countries in East Asia. The 'pivot', or rebalancing, towards Asia, as framed under the US administration of Barack Obama since 2011, is a case in point.

While tensions originating from the Cold War remain a rationale to keep US alliances intact in North-East Asia, this is less the case in South-East Asia, particularly in Thailand and the Philippines, both of which are traditional US allies. While American troops have remained in both Japan and Korea, they withdrew from the Philippines in 1992. The withdrawal from Thailand happened in 1976 following the end of the Vietnam War.

Even in South-East Asia, there seems to be different approaches between the two traditional allies. The South China Sea disputes represent clear and present danger for the Philippines, which, until the election of President Rodrigo Duterte, helped cement its alliance with the United States. Thailand, meanwhile, is an uneasy ally for the United States owing to the fact that both countries share fewer common threats and that Thailand also has close ties with China.

Accordingly, this chapter argues that Thailand represents the most obvious case of an ally at the crossroads in Asia. This can be seen as Thailand tends to pursue a hedging strategy towards several major powers rather than sticking to any single great power. Having no territorial dispute with China, bilateral ties are strengthening between Thailand and China. Thailand thus epitomises a test case for the United States regarding the extent to which it can succeed in managing its alliances in the 21st century.

This chapter first examines how the US–Thailand alliance evolved, focusing on the post–Cold War era. It then explores the changing international environment and the current perspectives of the alliance. It does so by exploring the opportunities and costs of the alliance today, which are punctuated by the outstanding factors of the rise of China and the current Thai political crisis that has continued since 2005. The chapter contends that, while management of the US–Thailand alliance is at a difficult point in its development, it is not impossible, given the two countries share some interests on regional stability and non-traditional security, which is underpinned by interoperability and the existence of a traditional/institutionalised relationship between the two nations.

Origin of the US–Thailand Alliance

Thailand (then known as Siam) became America's first diplomatic partner in Asia when the two states signed the Treaty of Amity and Commerce in 1833. Though focusing on commercial relations, not security, the treaty well served the purposes of both countries. While Siam could diversify its relations with Western powers as a strategy to avoid colonisation by

European powers, the United States obtained access to mainland South-East Asia that was equal to that of the European nations then operating in the region.[1]

The circumstances of the current US–Thailand alliance can be traced back to the end of World War II, when Washington came to defend Thailand from its status as a defeated country. As Britain launched numerous demands on Thailand, which initially sided with Japan during the war, the United States argued that Thailand was not a unitary state during wartime, as several internal Free Thai Movements supported the allied powers against the Japanese. This created the pretext for trust between the two nations. But it wasn't until the intensification of the Cold War that the alliance was formalised, first by the 1954 Manila Pact, which formed the Southeast Asia Treaty Organization (SEATO) and, second, through a communiqué signed by Thailand's Foreign Minister Thanat Khorman and US Secretary of State Dean Rusk in 1962. The purpose of the Thanat–Rusk communiqué was to seek Thailand's cooperation to prevent the spread of communism in Laos, but it is always cited as the basis for alliance, which culminated in nine joint military bases.

Various assistance and infrastructure-building schemes, supported by both the United States and the World Bank, were arranged as a result of the alliance. Most prominent among these were military facilities including the US-built airfields at U-Tapao, a deep-water port at Suttahip and the Mittraparb Highway to the hinterland north-eastern provinces. Investment from the private sector also thrived. Importantly, the two countries signed the Treaty of Amity and Economic Relations in 1966, which gave Americans privileges in doing business in the kingdom, where the prevailing conditions for foreign investment were restrictive. Specifically, the treaty allows American citizens and businesses incorporated in the United States, or in Thailand, to maintain a majority shareholding or to wholly own companies in Thailand, and thereby engage in business on the same basis as would a Thai national.[2]

1   Catharin Dalpino, 'The United States–Thailand Alliance: Issues for a New Dialogue', *NBR Special Report*, no. 33, The National Bureau of Asian Research, Oct. 2011, p. 4.
2   American companies are also exempt from most of the restrictions on foreign investment imposed by the Foreign Business Act of 1999.

The alliance weakened when the United States withdrew from the Vietnam War in 1973 and eventually vacated the joint bases in Thailand in 1976. In fact, from 1973–76, Thailand briefly enjoyed a more liberal political atmosphere whereby anti-base protests periodically occurred. Thai leaders, meanwhile, came to view American military presence as an increasing liability. At any rate, Washington was not willing to maintain American troops on mainland South-East Asia. With the communist takeover of the Indochina states, Thailand was left in the cold. When the threat from Vietnam was looming large after its invasion and subsequent occupation of Cambodia in late 1978, Bangkok had to seek help from Beijing instead (further discussed below). Later, Thailand came to limit US military access to facilities following the 1975 Mayaguez Incident, when the United States decided to take action unilaterally. The incident started with the seizing of the American container ship *Mayaguez* by the Khmer Rouge. The United States reacted by sending military operations from the U-Tapao air base in Thailand without consulting Bangkok.[3]

Thai Perceptions of the United States

Thailand tends to view its alliance with the United States as a broad-based relationship, rather than one of security alone, which seems to be in contrast to America's view of the relationship.[4] Therefore, it is crucial to consider overall bilateral ties when analysing the alliance relationship. It is important to note that I refer to Thai perceptions at both the level of elites and the general public.

Though the general public is not well informed about the relationship with the United States, the media tends to reflect general feelings toward the United States. While Thai people will refer to the United States as *America maha-mit* (great friend America), the term is often used negatively and it tends to be followed by 'why does a great friend treat us like this?'. These views stem from a variety of American actions, ranging from economic disputes and pressures, and the US characterisation of Thailand as a country with poor standards in the areas of human rights, human trafficking, intellectual property and money laundering. In particular, the two countries' relations have been subject since the 1980s to difficulties

3   Lewis Stern, 'Diverging Roads: 21st Century US–Thai Defense Relations', *Strategic Forum*, no. 241, Jun. 2009, p. 1.
4   Dalpino, 'The United States–Thailand Alliance: Issues for a New Dialogue', 2011, p. 7.

arising from US economic pressure. Thais perceive that the United States has failed to appreciate the historical depth of the bilateral relationship and thus all too often fails to act in honour of the friendship rather than economic calculations and shifting policy interests.

These negative perceptions can be traced back to America's withdrawal in the 1970s. While the region was still facing threats of communism, the United States supported authoritarian regimes in Thailand. This left America open to criticism of its inconsistencies over democracy and human rights. Indeed, the left-leaning ideology of many Thai intellectuals led to their criticism of the United States in general and American capitalism more specifically. Importantly, under the influence of these outspoken opinion leaders in Thai society, it is relatively common for Thais to be critical of the United States. For example, a joint US–Thailand seminar that included senior politicians, bureaucrats, and leading academics in 2002 concluded that, in Thailand, there is 'deep mistrust of America'.[5]

Yet, most people who criticise the United States would prefer either visiting or sending their children to study there more than most other countries. Compared to most South-East Asians, the majority of Thais are relatively more receptive to American culture, ranging from Hollywood movies, American music, IT gadgets, fashion, and American lifestyle and consumption in general. In other words, feelings toward the United States are mixed: while there are commonly negative views about the US Government and corporations, most Thais are positive about American culture.

The Post–Cold War Events

After the end of the Cold War, several events strained the US–Thailand alliance during the 1990s. The first was Thailand's rejection of an American proposal to pre-position military equipment in Thailand's territorial waters in 1994. The second was the failure of an FA-18 jet fighter sale, when Bangkok decided to trim its military budget largely due to financial difficulties after the 1997 Asian financial crisis. The third was when the United States was found responsible for a chemical spill at Hua

---

5   John Brandon & Nancy Chen (eds), 'United States–Thailand Relations in the 21st Century', Bilateral Conference Summary, *The Asia Foundation*, 11–13 Mar. 2002, p. 3.

Hin airport in 1999.[6] In the same year, Thais were disappointed when US opposition was perceived as pivotal in Thailand's failed bid for the World Trade Organization presidency.

Likewise, three major events toward and during the late 1990s further qualified Thai attitudes toward the United States. First, the United States offered Thailand little support in response to the impact of the Asian financial crisis in 1997. Antagonism increased further as Western companies bought up Thai companies at fire sale prices. In contrast, regional powers like Japan and China engaged and cooperated with crisis-hit countries. For instance, Japan offered Thailand soft loans under the Miyazawa Initiative and China held back from devaluing its currency. This made it easier for other Asian countries to recover, particularly as export prices were increasing. In this regard, ASEAN+3 (ASEAN plus China, Japan and Korea) represented a significant regional cooperation scheme, fostering closer ties among regional powers and South-East Asian states, including Thailand.

Second, Thais were reluctant to support the unilateralism of the George W Bush administration, which produced policies such as America's failure to ratify the Kyoto Protocol, the war on terror and the invasions of Afghanistan and Iraq. Thai attitudes were further hardened by America's apparent lack of interest in the region, which was indicated by the consecutive absences of Secretary of State Condoleezza Rice from the annual ASEAN Regional Forum (ARF) meetings during the mid-2000s. Both events tarnished the US image for the Thais and other South-East Asians. This was very much in contrast with the image of China, which is seen as generously giving unconditional assistance to ASEAN countries. Following Bush's visit to Thailand in 2003 for the APEC Summit, however, the US–Thailand alliance was resurrected after Washington designated Thailand as a non-NATO ally. Despite Thai society's misgivings about the US-led war in Iraq in pursuit of its oil interests, the administration of Thaksin Shinawatra sent troops to support the US enterprise in Iraq. The aim was to predispose Washington to begin free trade agreement (FTA) negotiations with Thailand.

Third, Washington's suspension of assistance and criticism of Thailand following the military coup in 2006 further alienated many Thais. Elites who supported the coup charged Washington with failing to understand

---

6   Stern, 'Diverging Roads', 2009, pp. 3–4.

the context of the kingdom. Some went further and argued that Thai coups solved political deadlocks. Such arguments were made less vocally, however, after the coup further worsened the existing political crisis in the kingdom. Very few Thais understand Section 508 of the US Foreign Operations Appropriations Act, which prohibits providing funds to a foreign government deposed by decree or military coup. Overall, as Thailand's divisions deepened, feelings toward the United States became increasingly mixed. For instance, the anti-Thaksin groups (the yellow shirts) were happy that Thaksin at some point was barred from entering the United States, a position that outraged the Thaksin supporters (the red shirts). Any US statements regarding protests or violence in the nation were received differently by these two groups. Protest groups would be heartened by the airing of US concerns about human rights violations, believing that Washington's protests helped deter the government from ordering military crackdowns. The opposition, meanwhile, would not be happy with US criticism. In short, US action or inaction regarding the Thai political crisis was viewed negatively by one or other of the two sides of the Thai crisis.

The election of the Obama administration briefly restored America's image through its reengagement policy. Thais value high-level visits and Secretary of State Hillary Clinton's participation in the 2009 ARF summit in Thailand helped to improve the relationship. America's diplomatic efforts were warmly welcomed by several South-East Asian nations, against a backdrop of China's growing assertiveness in the South China Sea and the Mekong River. The territorial disputes over the Spratly and Paracel Islands made Vietnam and the Philippines particularly nervous, while concerns have been raised over China's construction of dams on the Mekong, since they affect countries downstream, like Laos, Cambodia, Vietnam and Thailand. It should come as no surprise then, that American initiatives such as the Lower Mekong – Mississippi Cooperation have been welcomed as an alternative to engaging with China. Accordingly, the American reengagement efforts, coupled with public diplomacy and strong American soft power, have gained much acceptance from South-East Asia. Overall, the Obama administration strengthened America's image in Thailand.

Following the 2014 coup, however, the United States showed even more hostile attitudes toward the military government. Washington responded to the coup with a series of criticisms and sanctions, including the threat to move Cobra Gold—the largest regional joint military exercise—

to Darwin.[7] Wary that such moves would only push Thailand further into Beijing's orbit, Washington sent its first high-level visit of Deputy Secretary of State Daniel Russell to the kingdom in early 2015. Yet the visit failed to improve relations after he made critical comments about the military junta during his speech at Chulalongkorn University. What further aggrieved the bilateral relationship was the 2015 Trafficking in Persons (TIP) Report, which saw Thailand drop down to 'Tier 3' category, falling even below Myanmar and Malaysia, both of which are allegedly involved in the ongoing Rohingya migrant problem either as a sending or receiving country.[8] Recently, US Ambassador Glyn Davies also made a strong comment in front of the media and directly to the Thai Foreign Minister over human rights violations, inviting the wrath of coup supporters. In this light, there seems to be the perception among the military and the Bangkok establishment that the United States is not supportive of Thailand's domestic politics.

With the new presidency of Donald Trump, the US–Thailand relations seems to be more nuanced. On the one hand, the Trump administration emphasises 'America First', showing the sign of less engagement to Asia and resulting in the end of the Obama's pivot strategy. Most ally countries in Asia are nervous if the alliances would be qualified. Trump's overall policy so far seems to be detrimental to American soft power and could downgrade the US image. On the other hand, Trump is less interested in democracy compared to his democrat predecessor. This can extend more space for the military government in Thailand, as the Trump government is not likely to pressure Thailand much to return to democracy. Evidently, following North Korea's frequent missile tests during the 2017 spring, Trump came to value the traditional allies in South-East Asia more by making personal phone calls to Prime Minister Prayut Chan-o-cha of Thailand, as well as the leaders of the Philippines and Singapore. President Trump also invited Prime Minister Prayut to visit him in Washington, DC. Overall, the US–Thailand relations can fluctuate, depending on political regimes and leadership changes.

---

7   Though Cobra Gold remained in Thailand, the exercises were downsized to about 10,000 personnel in 2015 and 8,500 in 2016 respectively. See Prashanth Parameswaran, 'US, Thailand Launch 2016 Cobra Gold Military Exercises Amid Democracy Concerns', *The Diplomat*, 9 Feb. 2016, viewed Jul. 2016, thediplomat.com/2016/02/us-thailand-launch-2016-cobra-gold-military-exercises-amid-democracy-concerns/.

8   The 2016 TIP Report recently ungraded Thailand to Tier 2. See 'Thailand Gets Upgraded in US TIP Report', *Bangkok Report*, 1 Jul. 2016, viewed Jul. 2016, www.bangkokpost.com/news/security/1024141/thailand-gets-upgraded-in-us-tip-report.

Thailand's Changing Security Environment

With a new security environment in the post–Cold War era, threats to Thailand's security primarily come from the border areas in the forms of drug and human trafficking.[9] In the 1990s, the Thai Government announced that the drug trafficking industry was a major threat to national security. Meanwhile, skirmishes over territorial disputes with Laos erupted briefly in 1987, and more recently with Cambodia. Border tensions with Myanmar used to be frequent, particularly between the Tatmadaw (Myanmar Armed Forces) and minority rebel groups along the border. Accordingly, Thailand embraced a comprehensive security approach, comprising of both traditional and non-traditional security.

An insurgency in Thailand's Muslim-majority south has continued since 2004. While Manila allowed thousands of American troops to deploy to help curb terrorism, based on the US–Philippines Visiting Forces Agreement that came into force in 1999, a similar move is unthinkable in Thailand, which would treat it as an infringement of sovereignty.

Since 2005, Thailand has been trapped in a prolonged political crisis. Leading to hundreds of causalities, the political crisis has been dogged by coups d'état, violent riots and military crackdowns. The controversy around former prime minister Thaksin Shinawatra continues.[10] Thailand's preoccupation with its protracted domestic conflicts inadvertently affects international relations, including the US alliance.

Another key security problem that arose toward the end of the last decade is a border dispute with Cambodia over Prea Vihear Temple. The United States was less likely to play a role in this dispute due to its cultivation of ties with countries such as Vietnam and Cambodia, including military aid. In fact, Thailand aired concerns over US–Cambodia joint exercises, arguing that it was undercutting the US–Thailand alliance.[11] Thailand perceives limited benefit from its US alliance on issues such as territorial disputes with neighbouring countries.

---

9   Panitan Watanayagorn, 'Thailand: The Elite's Shifting Conceptions of Security', in Muthiah Alagappa (ed.), *Asian Security Practice*, Stanford University Press, 1998, p. 438.

10   See Kitti Prasirtsuk, 'Thailand in 2015: Bill, Blast, and Beyond', *Asian Survey*, vol. 56, no. 1 (Jan./Feb. 2016), pp. 168–73. doi.org/10.1525/as.2016.56.1.168.

11   Dalpino, 'The United States–Thailand Alliance: Issues for a New Dialogue', 2011, pp. 10–11.

Given the changing threat environment, Thai perceptions of the US alliance are not favourable. At a closed-door brainstorming session on Thailand's strategies toward the United States and China in five years (2012–17), three dozen representatives from concerned agencies (e.g. the ministries of foreign affairs, defence, and commerce), the private sector and academia agreed unanimously that Thailand must look beyond the US alliance and strengthen engagement with China, even as they lamented the decreasing utility of their strategic ties with the United States, which fitted more with the Cold War, but not the contemporary milieu.[12]

In sum, threats to Thailand's security can be understood as either domestic, non-traditional, or traditional border disputes with neighbouring countries, all of which are less likely to see direct US involvement. More specifically, the United States does not have a major role in Thai security thinking. Bangkok also believes that Thai security is of increasingly marginal interest to the United States and that the alliance is less important compared to America's relationship with its other traditional allies in the Asia-Pacific—Japan, South Korea, Australia and the Philippines. Considering that the United States is increasingly cultivating security ties with Indonesia, Cambodia and Vietnam, commentators worry that Thailand is being relegated to the group of second-tier allies.[13] As regional developments define new interests for South-East Asian countries, Thailand will increasingly divert its security identity away from the United States.

The Rise of China

The rise of China attracts much attention in the 21st century. Though the fast-growing China was initially viewed as China Threat in the 1990s, since the 2000s, most countries have come to appreciate China as an opportunity, particularly on economic grounds. China's strategic interests have seen it cultivate bilateral relationships with many countries, and Thailand is no exception.

Since 2009, China has become Thailand's largest export market, surpassing the United States. By 2012, China replaced Japan as Thailand's top trade partner. In 2015, Thailand traded with China as much as 2.2 trillion baht

---

12 Kavi Chongkittavorn, 'Thailand Looks Beyond the US Alliance', *The Nation*, 2 Apr. 2012.
13 Conversation with Thai and Japanese professors, Bangkok, Feb. 2012.

(US$65 billion), which comprises 15 per cent of Thailand's total trade, compared to the 1.3 trillion baht (US$39 billion), or 9.1 per cent of Thailand's total trade, that it traded with the United States.[14] Though Japan has remained Thailand's top investor, Chinese investments are steadily increasing. Importantly, Chinese from mainland China represent the number one source of tourists in the kingdom, as many as 7.9 million (26.5 per cent of total tourists) in 2015.[15]

For Thailand, in fact, the turn to China is not a recent phenomenon. Since the late 1970s, when Vietnam invaded Cambodia and American troops left mainland South-East Asia, it was essential for Thailand to seek help from China. As the frontline state, Thailand was concerned at incursions by Vietnamese forces, particularly when they crossed the Thai border to hunt down the Khmer Rouge. Beijing responded by sending support to the anti-Vietnam Khmer Rouge as well as cutting assistance to the underground Thai Communist Party. And, as China waged a border war with Vietnam in early 1979, the Vietnamese military shifted to the north. This changed the shape of regional defence realities and formed the basis for the Sino–Thai alliance. A wide range of arms sales at 'friendship prices' was offered to Thailand, including armoured vehicles, artillery and missiles.[16] This pattern of the Sino–Thai alliance continued despite the two coups in Thailand in 2006 and 2014. When the United States placed sanctions on Thailand after the 2006 coup, especially in terms of security cooperation, China offered Thailand good deals on arms purchases and other forms of assistance and cooperation. Notably, the Chinese provided US$49 million in military assistance, almost double the size of the US$24 million in US military assistance that was legally suspended in accordance with Section 208 mentioned above.[17]

The Thai political crisis and the two coups should not be exaggerated as the major reason for Thailand to lean toward China. The trend has been that way regardless of who is in government in Bangkok, whether elected or non-elected. Economic interests with China represent a strong incentive for any Thai Government to strengthen the relations

---

14 Ministry of Commerce, Trade Information, www.moc.go.th/index.php/moc-english.html# (accessed July 2016).
15 Department of Tourism, 'Million of Tourists', viewed Jul. 2016, www.tourism.go.th/view/2/Million%20of%20Tourists/EN-US.
16 Walter Lohman, 'Reinvigorating the US–Thailand Alliance', *Backgrounders*, no. 2609 (26 Sep. 2011), p. 8. See also Stern, 'Diverging Roads', 2009, p. 2.
17 Stern, 'Diverging Roads', 2009, p. 3.

with China. The Thaksin government (2000–05) and the Yingluck government (2011–14) opposed the Thai military and sought to cultivate ties with China, ranging from free trade agreements, the lease of pandas, arms purchases and frequent high-level visits. The 2014 coup and the subsequent US antagonism only accelerated Thailand's gravitation towards China.

More recently, China continues to tempt ASEAN and other Asian nations with even bolder initiatives. The Asian Infrastructure Investment Bank (AIIB) and the Belt and Road Initiative are two examples, aimed at building and upgrading infrastructure to increase connectivity in Asia. Recent train deals with Laos, Thailand and Indonesia represent efforts in this regard, which will contribute to the goal of ASEAN connectivity that was initially proposed and advocated by Bangkok. Beijing also recently proposed the Lancang–Mekong Cooperation Initiative to further cooperation among Mekong River riparian countries. The aim has not only been to ameliorate tensions and concerns over China's dam construction, which significantly affects the downstream countries, but also to counterbalance the Lower Mekong – Mississippi Cooperation, as proposed by the United States. In addition, China and ASEAN are negotiating the Regional Comprehensive Economic Partnership (RCEP), a pan-regional trade arrangement that also involves Japan, Korea, India, Australia and New Zealand. In short, compared to the United States, China's engagement appears to have more relevance to the interests of South-East Asia and Thailand.

In 2012, Thailand and China elevated their relations to a comprehensive strategic partnership. Since then, both sides have been steadily following the plan through various schemes of cooperation and exchanges, including frequent high-level visits, exchange of personnel in commander and staff colleges, joint seminars and so on. Importantly, both countries have expanded the Strike military exercises to cover army and also, recently, air force.

Thailand, therefore, arguably has the closest relationship with China, compared to other South-East Asian nations. Short of a territorial dispute with China, the relationship has been cordial. For instance, Thailand is the first country in South-East Asia to host leased pandas from China since 2003. In the so-called 'Panda Diplomacy', China leases pandas to only a limited number of countries to signify the importance of relations. Furthermore, in April 2012, Thailand's Defence Minister led a military mission, including chiefs of army, navy and air force, to China and paid a courtesy call to the then Vice President Xi Jinping. Such visits are rare and, in the current military government, Prime Minister Prayut has visited China several times, while Defence Minister Prawit Wongsuwan has met with high-level defence counterparts on many occasions.

Risk Factors in Gravitating Towards China

While there is good news about Sino–Thai relations, there are also several risks, and key infrastructure projects are a case in point. Thailand's railway project with China has become problematic. Initially, the Thai Government was optimistic about upgrading its outdated train system by developing medium- and high-speed railway lines with China. As negotiations dragged on, Thailand increasingly found that China was a demanding partner, particularly compared with other offers from Japan. For instance, China would charge higher interest rates on its loans—at almost 4 per cent, compared to 0.5–1.5 per cent for Japan. On operational management, China's offers were also demanding and imposed stringent rules relating to technological transfer, which again contrasted with those of the Japanese. Considering Thai leaders' general positive sentiments toward China, the inability for the railway project to move forward was disappointing.

Second, similar to other South-East Asian states like Myanmar and Laos, Thailand is increasingly exposed to economic threats from China. For instance, Chinese capitalists are purchasing large plots of land through their connections with Thai nominees. Real estate projects are constructed to cater for Chinese customers, and revenue from Chinese tourism flows to Chinese nationals via their travel agencies, restaurants and tour guides. While Chinese students are heavily represented at Thai universities, many never return to China after graduation. Overall, China represents both opportunities and threats for Thailand.

Third, the South China Sea disputes between China and some ASEAN members—the Philippines, Vietnam and Malaysia—constitutes a risk factor for Thailand–China relations. Though Bangkok may be able to play a coordinator role, as it did constructively during its assignment as China–ASEAN country coordinator during 2012–15, the situation is escalating. Sporadic tensions in US–China and Japan–China relations also raise concerns for ASEAN countries, including Thailand. Both issues signify that it is not plausible to lean toward China too much.

Whither the US–Thailand Alliance?

With negative attitudes towards the United States prevalent in Thailand, it is difficult to develop a common thread of strategic thinking between the two countries. In principle, Thailand maintains the alliance relationship with the United States, as exemplified by the number of annual military cooperation initiatives in which it is involved, including Cobra Gold and more than 50 other bilateral and multilateral exercises. Operationally, the Thai military command structure, weapons and overall interoperability remains highly compatible with US forces.

In practice, however, Thailand, cautiously responding to America's pivot, sees the United States as a difficult ally to work with. Several events point to that direction. The Yingluck government significantly delayed approval of the usage of the U-Tapao air base for the SEAC4RS (Southeast Asia Composition, Cloud, Climate Coupling Regional Study) in 2012. There was a concern that the project might raise some suspicion from China about US spying activities using the Thai air base. Likewise, the current military government under Prayut Chan-o-cha rejected a US aircraft basing request in 2015.[18] This was in stark contrast to earlier Thai responses to US calls to use the base for humanitarian assistance and disaster relief (HADR) in the case of the 2004 tsunami, the 2008 Cyclone Nargis, as well as the 2015 Nepal earthquake. Thailand still cooperates with the United States, but tends to steer military exercises and cooperation more towards HADR, so as not to make China unhappy. In short, Thailand responded to the American pivot with considerable reluctance.[19]

To the disappointment of the United States, such reluctance was felt despite the fact that Bangkok and Washington have just signed the Joint Vision Statement for the Thai–US Defense Alliance in 2012. Emphasising the 21st-century security partnership, the joint statement aims to

---

18   Prashanth Parameswaran, 'Thailand Mulls New US Aircraft Basing Request', *The Diplomat*, 28 May 2015, viewed Jul. 2016, thediplomat.com/2015/05/thailand-mulls-new-us-aircraft-basing-request/.

19   See Kitti Prasirtsuk & William Tow, 'A Reluctant Ally? Thailand in the U.S. Rebalancing Strategy', in William Tow & Douglas Stuart (eds), *The New U.S. Strategy towards Asia*, Routledge, 2015.

reinvigorate the alliance and update the half-century-long Thanat–Rusk communiqué, which has always been cited as the cornerstone of the US–Thailand alliance. Specifically, the new statement calls for a partnership for regional security in South-East Asia, stability in the Asia-Pacific region and beyond, bilateral and multilateral interoperability and readiness, as well as relationship-building, coordination and collaboration at all levels. As it turned out, the 2012 joint statement falls short of the aim of cementing alliance relations.

Obviously, the status of the US alliance is not a current priority in Thai strategic thinking. In recent defence white papers, there is no clear mention of the US alliance and more emphasis is placed on ASEAN-led mechanisms and multiple partners.[20] The US arms previously acquired by the Thai military are ageing, a great many are nearing retirement, and there have been few recent purchases. Understandably, Thailand prefers less costly arms that come with technological transfer, and is trying to diversify its sources of purchase by approaching China, Ukraine, Sweden, Korea, Spain, Israel and Russia. The purchase of the Swedish Gripen, rather than the American F-series jet fighters, is indicative of this.

Though the developments discussed above may seem pessimistic, there are several promising factors for the future of the US–Thailand alliance. First, Thailand continues to have deep and long cooperation with the United States, particularly in terms of interoperability. China is no match in this regard. Regular military exercises and various forms of military cooperation have ultimately quietly and firmly institutionalised the US–Thailand alliance. Military-to-military relations remain robust with more than 50 joint US–Thailand exercises annually. Between 2001 and 2009, the total number of military exercises increased from 44 to 59, seven of which are multilateral.[21] Cobra Gold is not the only large-scale military exercise, but also Cope Tiger, the Red Flag (previously Cope Thunder), and CARAT (Cooperation Afloat Readiness and Training). While originally focusing on the navy, these bilateral exercises have expanded to cover the army and air force. The Americans also benefit from conducting

---

20   Thai Ministry of Defense, *Defense White Paper 2013*, p. 8.
21   John Baseel, 'The Military Relationship between Thailand and the United States in the Post September 11th Era', MA Thesis, Chiang Mai University, 2009, p. 52.

exercises in different terrain. In recent years, the exercises increasingly focus on counterterrorism, counterinsurgency, civil affairs, peacekeeping and, importantly, humanitarian assistance.[22]

US–Thai military relations can be attributed to the role of the Joint US Military Advisory Group Thailand (JUSMAGTHAI), which has been active in various schemes of military cooperation, particularly military exercises, humanitarian and counter-drug missions. In fact, JUSMAGTHAI organises one of the largest International Military Education and Training (IMET) programs for Thailand and a number of cadets will be sent to study in the United States each year. Likewise, American military officers are sent to Thailand's Command and General Staff Academy. The socialisation is helpful in pursuing more cooperation. Apart from the military-to-military relations, Thailand and the United States engage in bilateral strategic dialogue.

Second, Thailand is a workable partner. Thanks to the interoperability accumulated through years of military exercises, training and equipment purchase, a number of new cooperation initiatives are proceeding. In response to the increasing terrorism threats following the 9/11 terrorist attacks on the United States in 2001, Thailand has been host to a new multilateral naval exercise called SEACAT (South-East Asia Cooperation Against Terrorism) since 2002. This exercise aims to police South-East Asia's sea lanes for maritime terrorism and piracy. Importantly, Thailand's cooperation with the United States in arresting Hambali, a key Al-Qaeda member, in 2003 highlights the ability of the two countries to work effectively on non-traditional security issues.

Moreover, Thailand and the United States reached an agreement in late 2002 to create a war reserve stockpile,[23] the first US stockpile outside of NATO territories and South Korea.[24] This demonstrates a part of the cooperation under the non-NATO alliance.

Third, the areas of shared interests between the United States and Thailand remain considerable, specifically on regional stability and non-traditional security. The United States remains the most important actor

---

22   Baseel, 'The Military Relationship between Thailand and the United States in the Post September 11th Era', 2009, p. 53.
23   Memorandum of Agreement Concerning the Transfer of Equipment and Munitions from United States War Reserve Stocks to the Government of the Kingdom of Thailand, *Treaties and International Act Series 02-1126*.
24   Stern, 'Diverging Roads', 2009, p. 2.

in maintaining regional stability. Thailand relies on stable regional order to develop its country. So do other regional countries. Any cooperation toward that goal would be welcome. Admittedly, however, it may be harder to mutually agree on the appropriate kind of cooperation, and its extent, that would lead to regional stability.

In this regard, cooperation is increasingly focused more on non-traditional security, including drugs, terrorism and insurgency, all of which are important threats to Thailand. Here, information and intelligence sharing is crucial. In 2012, following a US travel warning, several bombs exploded in Thailand. Since then, the US army has been assisting Thailand in developing bomb-disposal skills.[25]

Meanwhile, Thailand has played a role in peacekeeping operations and HADR, both of which will raise the country's international profile. This is particularly true after its successful involvement in the peace processes in Cambodia and Timor-Leste. The frequent occurrence of disasters in the region also motivated Thailand to play a more active role in this area. As the United States continues to be a key player in such activities, there is room for joint operation, particularly on HADR.

Finally, Thailand traditionally tends to diversify ties with major powers. Accordingly, sour relations with the United States can be only temporary during this military government. Once Thailand returns to electoral democracy, scheduled for 2018, bilateral relations should improve.

Conclusion

In Thai strategic thinking, the status of the US alliance is not at its peak. Owing to this is the changing security environment and shifting economic equation following the rise of China. There are several downsides in the US–Thailand alliance, stemming from America's security identity, Thailand's increasing shared economic and political interests with China and domestic politics. The general trend is that Thailand's relations with China are on the rise, while those with the United States are in relative decline.

---

25   Conversation with US army officer, Bangkok, Feb. 2011.

Yet, the relationship with China does not have only upsides, but also downsides, including economic threats from Chinese capitalists as well as China's assertiveness, especially with regard to the South China Sea. Thailand's high expectation of China's generosity could be disappointed. Thailand cannot rely too heavily on China, but has to resort to the familiar strategy of hedging and diversifying ties with major powers.

Meanwhile, there are quite a few upsides in the US–Thailand alliance. Military-to-military interactions with the United States remain intact, thanks to a half-century of institutionalised relationships and interoperability. Thailand also has converging interests with the United States on regional stability and non-traditional security. HADR emerged as a promising field for cooperation between the two nations.

At any rate, the United States must accept the changing realities and concentrate on what the two countries can do, rather than aiming unrealistically towards common strategic thinking and action. Thailand is not likely to maximise the utility of its US alliance, but rather prefers to maximise its room for manoeuvring between major powers. Hedging and limited alignments remains the viable choice for small ally countries like Thailand.[26] As Thailand tends to view relations with major powers in various lights, the United States should not concentrate on the security realm but rather seek to engage with its ally in a multidimensional manner. Given the region's security, economic and political environment, alliance management has become more difficult but still manageable.

26   See John Ciorciari, *The Limits of Alignment: Southeast Asia and the Great Powers since 1975*, Washington DC: Georgetown University Press, 2010.

9

Poland as an Ally

Witold Rodkiewicz

By 2016, Poland had been a member of the North Atlantic Alliance for over 15 years. This is a sufficiently long period for a country to establish a track record as an ally. Even a cursory look at Poland's record reveals a number of distinctive features that characterise Polish attitudes towards, and behaviour within, the alliance. These distinctive features have been shaped by three factors: geopolitical location, historical memories and national political traditions.

The first factor is obvious: Poland is a borderline state. In the east it borders three states—Belarus, Ukraine and Russia—which are not members of the alliance, and whose trajectory of development since 1991 has increasingly diverged from the path chosen by Poland and other post-Communist nations in Central Europe. Institutionally and symbolically, this borderline became even sharper following Poland's entry into the European Union in 2004. Moreover, one of those states, Russia, is not only a nuclear great power but also a successor state and the legal continuator of the Soviet Union, the great power that, not so long ago, played the role of a regional hegemon. While in the early 1990s it was open to question how the ruling elite in Moscow would interpret its 'successor' role, by the time of Vladimir Putin's presidency, the 'revisionist' elements in foreign policy thinking of the Russian elite were becoming increasingly evident.[1]

---

1   See, for example, a perceptive analysis by F Splidsboel-Hansen, 'Past and Future Meet: Aleksandr Gorchakov and Russian Foreign Policy', *Europe–Asia Studies*, vol. 54, no. 3, 2002, pp. 377–96.

The second factor is that of historical memory, which contains several layers. The most recent is the experience of living in a state with limited sovereignty. For the politically active generation that was shaped by the Solidarity period, this involves a memory of the threats of Soviet military intervention that were used as a tool of political pressure by both Moscow and the Communist leadership in Warsaw. A deeper layer consists of memory of the neighbouring power's use of military aggression to bring about a swift destruction of the reconstituted Polish state in 1939. This is also associated with the experience of being 'abandoned' by the Allies. A still deeper layer is that of the experience of more than a century-long period of living under foreign rule, after the final partition of the Polish–Lithuanian Commonwealth at the end of the 18th century.

The third factor is the deep attachment to the right of self-determination both on an individual as well as a collective level as symbolised by the principle of the political culture of the First Polish–Lithuanian Commonwealth: *quod omnis tangit, ab omnibus approbari debet* (what concerns all, should be approved by all). The political establishment of post-Communist Poland internalised the so-called 'Giedroyc doctrine',[2] which claimed that preservation of independence by the new post-Soviet states that lie between Poland and the Russian Federation is a fundamental Polish long-term interest.

'Existential' Alliance

Those factors produced a set of attitudes that influenced the way Poland functioned as an ally. They included first of all the assumption that Polish membership of the alliance is not a luxury or a matter of choice but an 'existential' necessity. It is an axiom for the Polish political establishment as well as for public opinion that, given Poland's geopolitical location and her historical experience, external security guarantees are an absolute must. These convictions are reflected in high levels of public support for membership of the alliance from the time when Poland was entering the alliance up to the present moment. Moreover, the feeling of relative vulnerability and the historical experience of an 'ineffective alliance' produced a conviction that an alliance cannot be limited to mere 'paper' guarantees. Guarantees have to be backed by real military capabilities and the political will to use those

2   Jerzy Giedroyc (1906–2000) was the chief editor of an influential emigré monthly, *Kultura*, which was published between 1945 and 2006, first in Rome and later in Paris.

capabilities cannot be taken for granted but needs to be cultivated. Hence, Poland's interest not only in membership but in keeping the alliance in good shape—both organisationally and politically.

A 'Serious' Ally

Poland treats its membership of the alliance seriously. This is reflected in the fact that Polish defence expenditure, in terms of GDP percentage, never fell below the European average and, since 2009, it has stayed consistently above it. Although it is true that Poland has not been fulfilling the official NATO requirement to maintain defence spending at 2 per cent of GDP, it has never fallen much below that threshold (only in the crisis year of 2008 did it drop to 1.6 per cent). This is particularly striking when one takes into account that, in per capita terms, Poland is one of the poorest members of the alliance and, what is politically more relevant, the poorest among the Central European countries that form a natural reference point against which Polish society measures its standard of living. Moreover, in real terms Poland has consistently increased its defence expenditures—again with the exception of the crisis year of 2008 and of 2013—since it joined the alliance. This spike in defence spending has been especially pronounced in recent years: in 2014 it rose by 11.5 per cent and, in 2015, by an estimated 21.7 per cent. In this respect Poland has become a clear leader in the alliance, overtaken only by Lithuania and (in 2015) Luxembourg.[3]

The other demonstration of Poland's commitment to the alliance was its significant and consistent contribution to the military operations conducted either by the alliance or—as in the case of Iraq—by the United States and some of its allies. In Afghanistan, the Polish contingent that was present from 2002 until 2014 reached, at the maximum point of engagement—the so-called 8th Rotation from the end of October 2010 – 2,600 military personnel. Overall, over 28,000 Polish military personnel participated in the Afghan mission, suffering 45 casualties.[4] Polish forces

---

3   See Tables 2, 3 and 4, in NATO, *Financial and Economic Data Relating to NATO Defence. Defence Expenditure of NATO Countries (1990–2013)*, 10 Mar. 2011 (www.nato.int/cps/pl/natohq/news_107359.htm); and Table 3, NATO, *Defence Expenditures of NATO Countries (2008–2015)*, 28 Jan. 2016, viewed Aug. 2016, www.nato.int/cps/en/natohq/news_127537.htm.
4   Official information of the Polish Ministry of Defense, 'Podsumowanie Polskiego Udzialu w Misji ISAF', viewed Mar. 2016, do.wp.mil.pl/artykuly/aktualnosci/2015-01-05-podsumowanie-polskiego-udziau-w-misji-isaf.

also participated in the stabilisation mission in Iraq where, between 2003 and 2008, a Polish contingent served as the core of a Multinational Division, responsible for one of the four security sectors in Iraq. In the first years of deployment the size of the contingent hovered around 2,500. Overall over 15,000 Polish military participated in the Iraqi operations, suffering 22 casualties.[5]

Poland also has participated in alliance missions in the Balkans, contributing a battalion-size unit to the NATO Implementation Force (IFOR) mission in Bosnia and Herzegovina and the Kosovo Force (KFOR) mission in Kosovo. An important detail that should be emphasised is that Polish contingents operated both in Iraq and in Afghanistan with relatively few restrictions (so-called 'national caveats'), which did not preclude their participation in combat operations.

Proving Commitment

Significant Polish participation in two major, costly and high-risk operations (Iraq and Afghanistan) throws an important light on Poland's approach to its alliances. Polish public opinion was opposed to Poland's participation in both operations—in particular in Iraq. This was due to the widespread perception that in both cases no direct Polish national security interest was involved. Poland had no major interest in the Middle East and did not see the Saddam Hussein regime as a particular security threat. Similarly, in the case of Afghanistan, the reaction of the Polish public was shaped by the fact that Poland has never been a target of terrorist attacks and radical Islam was not seen as an immediate threat to Polish security. On the contrary, the heavy involvement of the United States (in Iraq) and of NATO (in Afghanistan) in out-of-area operations was seen as running directly against Polish security interests, since it was diverting US/NATO resources and attention from preparations for the Article 5 contingencies on the Eastern flank of the alliance.

Nevertheless, the decisions to participate in those operations were meant to demonstrate Poland's commitment to its allies and to the alliance. This was bound up with expectations—that some would describe as

5   P Hudyma, 'Udział Wojsk Polskich w Misjach Zagranicznych o Charakterze Pokojowym i Stabilizacyjnym, w Latach 1953–2008', PhD Thesis, Adam Mickiewicz University, Poznań, 2011, p. 98.

naïve—that in this way Poland was creating political and moral 'IOU-notes' that could be 'cashed in' when Poland is faced with an actual military threat.

America's 'Trojan Horse'

Poland's decision to send military forces to Iraq highlights another important strand in the Polish approach to the alliance. NATO is perceived first of all as an institutional framework that provides Poland with a security guarantee from the United States. This 'America-centric' approach has a persuasive pragmatic rationale that is connected with the point already mentioned above—the 'existential' nature of the alliance for Poland. Since the alliance is seen as an instrument for providing real military assistance in case of aggression, the gradual and consistent demilitarisation of Western Europe that could be observed after the end of the Cold War, meant that the United States has been the only player that realistically could be expected to have sufficient forces at its disposal to offer significant assistance that would be effective in military terms. Moreover, the United States was credited with greater willingness to use military force than West European nations, and therefore less likely to hesitate when faced with the perspective of deployment that could involve real combat and carry the risk of an escalation into a large-scale conflict.

Therefore, Poland has always been eager to develop bilateral defence ties with Washington, beyond and outside the multilateral NATO framework. This is also why Warsaw decided to back Washington over the Iraq issue, even though this decision put it on a collision course with Germany and France, the two most influential EU states, and even though Poland was then in the process of negotiating its membership of the European Union.[6] Similarly Poland, after some hesitation and hard bargaining, signed and ratified in August 2008 a bilateral agreement with the United States allowing for the stationing of elements of the American anti-ballistic missile system in Poland.[7] It is important to note that the bargaining was about the degree to which the project was to be accompanied by

---

6   On the motives behind the decision, see, M Wągrowska, 'Udział Polski w Interwencji Zbrojnej i Misji Stabilizacyjnej w Iraku', *Raporty i Analizy*, no. 12, Warsaw: Center for International Relations, 2004, pp. 6–11.
7   M Wągrowska, 'Tarcza Antyrakietowa z Polskiej Perspektywy', in Amerykańska tarcza antyrakietowa w Europie, konieczność, warunki, akceptacja, Konrad Adenauer Stiftung, 2008, pp. 39–47.

development of other military ties. In effect, Poland was trying to utilise the missile defence project for developing a broader bilateral security relationship with the United States. The Polish aim was to get 'American boots' on the ground—a significant and permanent US military presence to guarantee that any military attack on Poland would inevitably mean a direct attack on the American armed forces.

A Recalcitrant Ally

The Polish–American bargaining that preceded the August 2008 agreement on the location of elements of the anti-missile shield in Poland demonstrated another distinctive feature of Polish alliance behaviour. Poland, due to its size, population and history, aspires to be a 'middling power' that is capable of articulating and defending its national interests within the alliance. It seeks to express its own vision for the alliance and expects to have its voice heard and taken into account, especially on those aspects of alliance policy that are directly relevant to the alliance's Eastern flank.

A few cases can be cited where Warsaw demonstrated that it was not about to accept the prevailing winds from Washington but would behave according to its own analysis of the strategic situation. The first such example was the Polish decision not to follow the tendency in the alliance, that was prevalent until the Russian military aggression against Ukraine in 2014, to restructure the military for expeditionary, out-of-area tasks, de-emphasising—and in some cases completely getting rid of—assets and capabilities necessary for conventional territorial defence. Poland tried to keep the balance, retaining a significant land warfare component armed with heavy equipment. Moreover, during the discussions preceding the adoption of the New Strategic Concept at the 2010 Lisbon summit, Poland—together with Norway—argued for retention of the Article 5 tasks (i.e. collective defence of member states' territories) being given sufficient weight and priority.[8]

Warsaw has consistently raised, almost from the beginning of its membership of the alliance, the issue of the lack of significant military presence and infrastructure on the territory of new members, as well as

---

8   See, for example, B Górka-Winter & M Madej (eds), *NATO Member States and the New Strategic Concept: An Overview*, Warsaw: Polish Institute of International Affairs, 2010, pp. 79–82.

a lack of contingency plans for their defence in case of military aggression. This was apparently met with a distinct lack of enthusiasm in both Berlin and Washington. In view of their assessment of Russian intentions and capabilities, such plans were redundant, while they might hamper the pursuit of cooperation with Russia by contradicting the official NATO line that it did not perceive Russia as a potential enemy. Nevertheless, Poland's persistence, facilitated by the Russian military operation against Georgia, in demanding contingency plans in case of an attack on Polish territory led to such plans being drawn up between 2008 and 2010.[9] Poland also was trying to persuade the alliance to hold military exercises on its territory that would not be limited to peacekeeping or crisis management operations but would prepare for Article 5 contingencies.

Conclusion

Poland's exposed strategic location, combined with its historical memories, has shaped its distinctive approach to the NATO alliance. The alliance is seen as an indispensable means of providing a military guarantee shielding the country from military pressure or even military aggression from the Russian Federation. Therefore, Poland attaches particular importance to the cultivation of transatlantic military links, both within the framework of NATO as well as bilaterally. Its primary interest was in the collective defence function of the alliance as opposed to crisis management and out-of-area operations. Nevertheless, it actively participated in out-of-area stabilisation operations conducted by its allies, deploying significant forces for extended periods of time, in order to prove its value as an ally and to accumulate a stock of good will and trust in allied capitals—first of all in Washington—that could be 'called in' in an hour of need. While demonstrating its alliance loyalty, Poland has at the same time revealed itself to be capable of hard bargaining, asserting its own interests within the alliance and of articulating a distinctive position on alliance policy based on its own, independent analysis of the strategic situation.[10]

9   B Klich, 'NATO po Afganistanie', in Piętnaście lat Polski w NATO, Warszawa, 2014, p. 121.
10   See, for example, R Kupiecki, 'The Security Dilemma Facing Central and Eastern Europe, NATO, the United States, and Transatlantic Security Relations', in R Kupiecki & A Michta (eds), Transatlantic Relations in a Changing European Security Environment, Warsaw: Center for Strategic and International Studies, 2015, pp. 73–74, 76.

Contributors

Youngshik Bong is a visiting research fellow at the Asan Institute for Policy Studies. Previously, Dr Bong was an assistant professor in the School of International Service at American University in Washington, DC and a Freeman postdoctoral fellow at Wellesley College and an assistant professor of Korean studies at Williams College. His research interests include the interplay between nationalism and security issues such as historical and territorial issues in East Asia, anti-Americanism and the RoK–US Alliance. He is the author of 'Past is Still Present: The San Francisco System and a Multilateral Security Regime in East Asia', *Korea Observer* (2010), and co-editor of *Japan in Crisis: What It Will Take for Japan to Rise Again?* (with TJ Pempel, The Asan Institute for Policy Studies, 2012). Dr Bong received his BA in political science from Yonsei University and his MA and PhD in political science from the University of Pennsylvania.

HDP (David) Envall is a research fellow in the Coral Bell School of Asia Pacific Affairs, The Australian National University, and an honorary associate at La Trobe University. His research focuses on Japanese security and foreign policy, political leadership and international relations in the Asia-Pacific.

Nina Græger has a PhD in political science (University of Oslo, 2007) and is Senior Research Fellow at the Norwegian Institute of International Affairs (NUPI), where she was also head of department (2008–13); and Associate Professor II in international relations at the Norwegian University of Life Sciences (2013–). She has published extensively on security, defence, interorganisational relations, military sociology and Norwegian foreign policy. Græger has served on various commissions appointed by the government, including the Advisory Council for Disarmament and Security Affairs (1997–2005) and the Conscription

Commission evaluating Norway's future military service (2014–15), and was personal political adviser (1996) to the Minister of Energy and Industry, Jens Stoltenberg.

Markus Kaim is Senior Fellow in the International Security Division of the German Institute for International and Security Affairs—Stiftung Wissenschaft und Politik (SWP). He has taught and held fellowships at universities on both sides of the Atlantic: as DAAD Professor for German and European studies at the University of Toronto (2007–08); as acting professor for foreign policy and international relations at the University of Constance (2007); as visiting fellow at the American Institute for Contemporary German Studies/Johns Hopkins University (2005); as adjunct professor at the Department for Political Science, University of Zurich (since 2012); and as guest instructor at the Hertie School of Governance, Berlin (since 2012).

Kristian Søby Kristensen is Deputy Director and Senior Researcher at the Centre for Military Studies at the University of Copenhagen. His research interests include Danish foreign and defence policy, European security and alliance politics as well as Arctic security.

Kristian Knus Larsen is Researcher at the Centre for Military Studies at the University of Copenhagen. He earned his PhD in political science from the University of Copenhagen and he has taught at the Baltic Defence College and presented graduate courses in public administration, security studies and strategy.

Wrenn Yennie Lindgren is a Research Fellow at NUPI, where she specialises in international relations in East Asia, the politics and foreign policy of Japan, East Asian states' interests in the Arctic, and traditional and non-traditional security issues in the Asia-Pacific region. She holds master's degrees in international policy studies (Monterey Institute of International Studies, United States) and Asia and Middle East studies (University of Oslo) and is a PhD candidate in international relations at Stockholm University.

Kitti Prasirtsuk teaches international relations at the Faculty of Political Science and serves as Director at the Institute of East Asian Studies, Thammasat University, Bangkok. He is appointed to the strategic committee to the Deputy Prime Minister and the Minister of Defense. Kitti also serves on the advisory committee for the Asia Centre under the Japan Foundation, which promotes exchange between Japan and ASEAN. Kitti received his BA from Thammasat, an MA from Keio University,

Japan, and a PhD from the University of California, Berkeley (2001). His areas of interest include international relations in East and South-East Asia, Japanese politics and foreign policy, and ASEAN. His current research is on soft power in East Asia.

Witold Rodkiewicz has an MA in history from Warsaw University (1985) and a PhD in history from Harvard University (1996). He is an analyst in the Centre for Eastern Studies (OSW) in Warsaw and an Adjunct Professor at the Centre for East European Studies at the University of Warsaw. His main research interests are Russian foreign policy and political thought.

Brendan Taylor is Head of the Strategic and Defence Studies Centre at The Australian National University. He is a specialist on great power strategic relations in the Asia-Pacific. His work has appeared in such leading international outlets as *Survival*, *The Washington Quarterly*, *The Pacific Review*, *International Affairs*, *Review of International Studies*, *Global Asia*, *Contemporary Southeast Asia*, *The Asan Forum*, *Asian Politics and Policy*, *Australian Journal of International Affairs*, *Asian Security* and the *Review of International Studies*. He is the author or editor of eight books including, most recently, *Australia's American Alliance* (Melbourne University Press, 2016).

William T Tow is Professor of international relations at The Australian National University's Coral Bell School for Asia Pacific Affairs. He was head of the school's Department of International Relations from 2011–15. Tow has authored/edited over 20 volumes and 100 journal/book articles on alliance politics, Asia-Pacific security issues and regional order building. He has been principal investigator in two major projects for the MacArthur Foundation's Asia Security Initiative. He has also been the editor of the *Australian Journal of International Affairs* and has served on the Foreign Affairs Council, Australian Department of Foreign Affairs and Trade; and the National Board of Directors, Australian Fulbright Commission. Professor Tow has been a visiting fellow at Stanford University, IISS London and both the ISEAS Yusof Ishak Institute and Rajaratnam School of International Studies (ISIS) in Singapore.

Michael Wesley is Professor of international affairs and Dean of the College of Asia and the Pacific at The Australian National University. His research interests include Australian foreign policy, Asian security dynamics, state-building interventions and transnational security threats.

www.ingramcontent.com/pod-product-compliance
Lightning Source LLC
Chambersburg PA
CBHW040152270326
41927CB00034B/3431